Joseph Berington

The History of the Lives of Abeillard and Heloisa

Joseph Berington

The History of the Lives of Abeillard and Heloisa

ISBN/EAN: 9783741197840

Manufactured in Europe, USA, Canada, Australia, Japa

Cover: Foto ©Thomas Meinert / pixelio.de

Manufactured and distributed by brebook publishing software
(www.brebook.com)

Joseph Berington

The History of the Lives of Abeillard and Heloisa

Joseph Berington

The History of the Lives of Abeillard and Heloisa

THE

HISTORY

OF THE

LIVES

OF

ABEILLARD and HELOISA;

COMPRISING A PERIOD OF EIGHTY-FOUR YEARS

From 1079 to 1163.

WITH THEIR GENUINE

LETTERS,

FROM THE COLLECTION OF AMBOISE.

A NEW EDITION.

Perfonne n'eft obligé d'écrire l'hiftoire ; mais quiconque
l'entreprend s'engage à dire la vérité toute entiere.

FLEURY. DISC. 4.

By the Rev. JOSEPH BERINGTON.

VOLUME I.

BASIL:

Printed and fold BY J. J. TOURNEISEN,

· MDCCXCIII.

ADVERTISEMENT.

$T HE$ indulgence with which the public has received the History of Abeillard and Heloifa, induces me to venture on this second edition. I have made no alterations in the work itself; because the expediency of doing it was not fuggefted even by the critics. But I have prefixed an Introduction of fome length, containing a general view of that part of the eleventh century, which had preceded the period I defcribed. It will be given gratis to the purchafers of the firft edition. The whole volume I now mean fhould be an Introduction to the hiftory of the fucceeding periods, which I purpofe, at

ADVERTISEMENT.

my leisure, to carry down to the beginning of the sixteenth century. It comprises three hundred and fifty years. Two large volumes, I hope, will contain the whole, which shall be published separately.

THE

PREFACE.

THE Hiflory of the Lives of Abeillard and Heloifa, which I now offer to the public, has, in fome fenfe, been the work of many years. No one has ever read Mr. Pope's inimitable poem, without being interefted in the fate of the lovers, whofe fad and tender ftory, he, as a poet, has told fo well. This intereft I felt, and I was prompted to inquire more into the real hiftory of their lives. The firft annals of the church, I could meet with, foon gave me the information I wanted, and I found that the general impreffion made by the poet's tale was not to be relied on. Abeillard, I faw, had not one trait of the character, he had portrayed ; and that Heloifa merited a much more favorable delineation. I alfo difcovered that they were great and confpicuous perfonages,

a 3

who had commanded the attention of the age, and
whofe virtues their contemporaries even had been
careful to celebrate. I then viewed the other
characters, and the general events of the period,
in which they lived, and they were interefting
I faw, and momentous. Should I ever become
an author, I thought, I would attempt *the
Hiftory of the Lives of Abeillard and Heloifa.* —-
My motives then are laudable.

At a time, when truths of every kind are fo
eagerly invefligated, and thofe of hiftory in particular, I have chofen a dark period; and if I can
bring it before the public in any form that may
raife attention, my defign will be fatisfied. I own,
I have fome confidence in the impofing names of
Abeillard and Heloifa. — The learned reader
muft not expect to find any thing abfolutely new.
Where was I to look for novelty in the records of
the eleventh and twelfth centuries? But as I have
taken the liberty to form my own judgment on
the characters and facts, I have defcribed, it may
be that, fometimes, I fhall feem to fuggeft new
ideas, or to prefent an old object in a new point
of view. It will be well, if fome critics may not

think it would have been better, I had adhered
more religiously to fome opinions, which age
feems to have fanctioned . I would have done it,
could I have been prevailed on to believe that
our anceflors were not men, open to prejudice
and falfe impreffions. There are circumftances,
when it is rather advantageous to be placed at
fome diftance from an object. Its light is not fo
dazzling, the medium is lefs troubled, and the
eye of the fpectator is more ferene and fteady.
What errors has not the cool fagacity of modern
criticifm corrected in the too credulous annals
of former times?

In writing the prefent hiftory I had then more
in view, than the bare delineation of the two
principal characters: but of thefe I have never
loft fight. It was impoffible, indeed, fo to draw
the events of the period together, as to make
them appear like branches from the leading object;
for, in their origin, they were not connected
with it. At any time, how little connexion has
the life of a literary man, and much lefs that of
a cloiftered nun, with the fchemes of politicians,
and the feats of warriors? What links, the

then difunited ftate of mankind threw into the events, I truft, I have not broken; and perhaps fome harmony of parts, and unity of defign, may be difcovered.

They who, from the title of my work, fhall expect the entertainment of a novel, will be difappointed. I profefs to give a genuine hiftory; and am I to blame, if Abeillard and Heloifa were not fo romantic, as the heroes of modern tales; or if their lives were lefs crowded with extraordinary and incredible adventures? Heloifa, however, will fometimes, I think, be able to keep pace with the wildeft flights of fancy. — But the reader muft be unconfcionably unreafonable in his expectations, who, whatever be his caft of character, 'fhall not find, in fuch a variety' of matter, fomething to gratify his curiofity. I have treated of love, religion, philofophy, politics, and war. The crufades are great events, and the characters of diftinguifhed men, but little known to the generality of readers, are doubtlefs interefting objects. — My inability to perfect fo various a plan I am not afhamed to own,

and in this fentiment, I can call more confid-
ently for indulgence.

A few years ago I tranflated, for my amufement,
the letters of Abeillard and Heloifa, and that
circumftance it was, which revived the idea,
I mentioned to have before entertained, of
writing their hiftory. The fources of information
were, I knew, genuine and abundant. I drew
them round me; and nothing remained but to
realize my favorite project. — The reader fhall
know what thefe fources were.

In 1616, was publifhed, for the firft time, at
Paris, a complete edition of Abeillard's works.
They had been collected with much care by
Francis d'Amboife, a great favorite in the courts
of Charles IX. and his brother Henry III. and
who gradually was promoted to offices of high
truft in the ftate. From his childhood, he fays [r],
he had been always fond of looking into old
libraries, and turning over dufty manufcripts.
In fome of thefe refearches he laid his hands on
the letters of Abeillard and Heloifa ; he read
them with much pleafure, and was induced to

[r] Praf. Apolog. p. 2.

purfue his inquiries. He found other works of
the fame author; but they were ill-written, and
not to be unravelled, without great labor. Nothing
can withftand the indefatigable toil of a true
antiquarian. Amboife procured other manufcripts:
he collated them together, and finally produced
one fair copy, which made ample compenfation,
he fays, for all the labor he had taken. Even
pofterity, he thinks, will be grateful to him, and
know how to value the pleafure and the profit,
they will derive from his refearches. With how
partial an eye, indeed, do we contemplate our
ówn, favorite purfuits!

Not fatisfied with the dear copy he poffeffed,
Amboife ftill wifhed to enlarge it. He applied to
different monafteries, and he again fearched the
libraries in Paris, and not without fuccefs. His
friends applauded his zeal, and gave him their
affiftance. His manufcripts fwelled to a large
bulk, and he read, arranged, and felected what
pleafed him beft. The rifing fun, he fays, often
found him at his tafk. So far fortune had
fmiled upon his labors, and he did not doubt
but foon he fhould be able to prefent the public

with the rich jewel he poffeffed. But little was
wanting to give it the laft finifh. Warm with
the idea, he went over to the Paraclet. The
abbefs, Madame de Rochefoucauld received him
with the greateft politenefs. He declared the
motive of his journey: fhe took him by the hand
and led him to the tomb of Abeillard and
Heloifa. Madame was his relation. Together they
examined the library of the abbey; and fhe
fhowed him many hymns, and prayers, and
homilies, written by their founder, which were
ftill ufed in their church [1].—Amboife then returned to Paris, and prepared his work for the
prefs.

As the reputation of his author, he knew, had
been much afperfed by fome contemporary
writers, he wifhed to remove the undeferved
ftigma, and to prefent him as immaculate, as
might be, before the eyes of a more difcerning
age. With this view he wrote a long *apologetic
preface*, which, he meant, fhould be prefixed to
the work. In this preface, a compofition inelegant
and affected, Amboife labors much to fhow that,

[1] Præf. Apolog. p. 6.

Abeillard was the greatest and best man, and
Heloisa the greatest and best woman, whom the
annals of human kind had recorded. He first,
very fairly, adduces the testimony of those, who
had spoken evil of them, whom he combats and
refutes. To these succeeds a list of their admirers.
He dwells on their every word, and gives more
weight to their expressions ; and the result is,
what we were prepared to expect from the pen of
Amboise. —The compilation, however, contains
some curious matter, and may be read with
pleasure. The antiquarian himself did not, I
believe, live to see his work before the public,
for it was not printed till the year 1616, and that,
as the king's licence expresses, by Nicholas
Buon.

The reader will find, in the course of the
following history, what this edition contains. The
letters form, by much, the most curious part, and
at the head of these is the *Historia Calamitatum*,
or, the *memoirs* of his own life, which Abeillard
wrote to a friend, and which I often quote. It
is indeed the only genuine repository, from

which many circumftances of his life can be
drawn.

To thefe *memoirs*, Andrew du Chefne, under
the affected appellation of *Querceianus*, wrote
illuftrative notes, which are fubjoined to Amboife's
collection. They are very curious, and often
throw great light on the fubject. — Du Chefne
lived in the laft century; and, from his great
refearches into the hiftory and antiquities of
France, he has deferved to be ftyled the father
of their hiftory. He and Amboife were friends.
Some critics have afcribed the whole edition of
the works of Abeillard to him; but without
fufficient foundation.

It is from the authors, quoted by Amboife in
his preface, or by Du Chefne in his notes, that I
have taken fome anecdotes, and many particular
circumftances, which, intentionally, I have never
failed to acknowledge. I could have no motive
for appearing ungrateful to my benefactors.

Modern writers, who fpeak of Abeillard, have
taken their materials from his memoirs, and I
was furprifed, on many occafions, to find them
fo inaccurate. His contemporaries treated him,

as they were affected by paffion, or intereft, or partiality, or truth, and their opinions have been varioufly copied. But there is very little to be collected from the writers of the age. They were too intent on difplaying the martial prowefs of their mafters, or on recording the extravagant pretenfions of the Roman pontiffs, or on blazoning the miraculous atchievements of their favorite faints, to attend to the comparatively uninterefting characters of more private life. Otho Frifingenfis, Geoffrey, a monk of Clairvaux, Bernard of Citaux, and Peter the venerable, abbot of Cluni, are the writers who principally mention Abeillard.

Bayle, among the moderns, a man of vaft abilities, but which he too often abufed to infult religion and to injure virtue, in his *Hiftorical and Critical Dictionary*, has entered very diffufely on the lives of Abeillard and Heloifa. Agreeably to his wonted practice he had read every thing, which hiftory had recorded of them, and all that he retails with the greateft profufion. In his notes he pours out his own obfervations, which are fometimes hazarded, and his criticifms, which are

not always juft. Whatever his teeming memory
could, on the occafion, fuggeft, he heaps together, and his prurient imagination runs to modern
anecdotes and ancient fables, in queft of obfcenity
and vulgar imagery. Modefly had never a more
determined adverfary to contend with. There is
much, I know, to be learned from this man;
but I would not look for pearls in a dunghill.
On the prefent occafion, he has been of little
ufe to me: the facts he relates, I could draw
from their fource, and I could not copy his loofe
digreffions, or his indecent allufions.__His ftrictures
on Heloifa are remarkably unjuft, and it is clear
that he wilfully mifreprefented her character.
Expreffions in her letters, which malevolence
may pervert, are to him demonftrations of her
guilt, and the language of confidence and fincerity
is the fpeech of meretricious impudence. — As his
own heart, probably, was infenfible to the impreffions of virtue, and he could not pity diftrefs,
I am not much furprifed at the indecency of *his*
remarks, and the general flippancy of *his* pen;
but that two clergymen of the church of England,

should have tranflated the moft exceptionable
paffages of his dictionary, and fhould have added,
by their tranflation, to their groffnefs, is not
quite fo pardonable. — I am not fufficiently
fevere either on Bayle or his tranflators.

In Moreri, or rather in the voluminous work
which goes under his name, the life of Abeillard
is very accurately given, as to its principal
incidents. Some miftakes there are, which might
have been eafily corrected, by more attention to
his own memoirs. — The more I have had
occafion to examine the works of others, the
more have I been convinced that hiftories, fuppofed
the moft authentic, are very little to be relied
on. Characters mifreprefented, dates miftaken,
and facts miftated, are then moft common,
when we look for accuracy, precifion, and truth.
The circumftance indeed is natural; for it is, on
thefe occafions, that the hiftorian is moft fwayed by
paffion, by party, by prejudice. When there is no
motive to miflead his judgment, or to bias his
will, he will deviate lefs, unlefs his negligence or
inattention be great: but in trifles, (if the bufinefs
of mankind can ever be fo denominated), it matters

little

little whether truth or falfhood preponderate. —
What really are the qualities to conftitute the
beft hiftorian, is hard to fay. To require that he
fhould be of no country, is requiring a thing
impoffible; and to fay that he fhould have no
religion, is a puerile demand. The philofophical
unbeliever is generally intolerant in his practice,
and always prejudiced in his ideas. The race has
been tried as hiftorians without fuccefs. Till a
man can be found without paffions, and then he
would be infipid; without prejudice, and then
he would want intereft; without party, and then
he would not be read; we muft be fatisfied
with fuch hiftorians as the common lot of humanity
can fupply, and read their writings, with the
fame indulgence, as we do a romance. If they
give us pleafure, it will be well; and the moft
fanguine author feldom looks for a better reward
to his labors. I mean not this as any apology for
my own work; for I profefs to be as accurate as
I can, and as truthful as the character of my
records will allow.

In 1720, the lives of Abeillard and Heloifa were
publifhed in two volumes at Paris. Dom Gervaife,

third abbot of la Trappe, is the author. He wrote them during his confinement at Notre-dame des Reclus, where he spent the fifty last years of his life. At the recommendation of de Rancé, first abbot of la Trappe, and who, worn down by austenties, had surrendered his charge, Dom Gervaise was elected to the important office. By nature headstrong and impetuous, bizarre in his humor, and singular in his maxims, (dispositions, which the incessant labor and dreadful rigors of the place had not corrected), he was ill-formed to conduct an institution, which demanded a man of peace, of prudence, of constancy of benevolence. The general regulations of the abbey he wished again to reform, and, as much as might be, to depart from the wise maxims of their founder. De Rancé saw the danger which threatened his new establishment, and he was yet able to avert it. Dom Gervaise, by an order from court, was dismissed. For some time, irritated and restless, he wandered from solitude to solitude, till, by another order, he was confined, as I just mentioned. Here, for he was a man of some abilities, and of much reading, he applied himself to the compilation of various works [1].

The work before me is written with care and honefty. Dom Gervaife had leifure, and he employed it in perufing the beft records. The ftyle is heavy, his reflections often uninterefting, and his periods loofe, negligent, and redundant. Though fo unhappily conftituted, as I defcribed him, ftill he had a mind, which was turned to piety, or he affected to appear religious and abftracted. In thefe difpofitions he viewed Abeillard as a great faint, and fuch he delineates his character, and Heloifa, his wife, was not, he thinks, a lefs perfect pattern of all the virtues. Dom Gervaife fhall fpeak for himfelf.

" Cet Abeillard fi connu, et en même tems
" fi inconnu, va donc paroitre au naturel dans
" cet ouvrage. On le verra né avec un bel
" efprit, capable des fciences les plus fublimes,
" devenu grand Philofophe malgré fes inclinations
" un peu trop tendres : la fin tragique de fon amour
" pour Héloife l'ayant conduit à une généreufe

[1] Dict. Hift.

" pénitence. Entré dans l'état monaflique, il y
" paroitra un des plus illuflres abbés de fon tems,
" & comme un martyr par l'auflérité de fa vie, &
" par les cruelles perfécutions qu'il fouffrit pour
" maintenir la difcipline réguliere. La grandeur
" de fon ame, fa patience héroique, éclatent dans
" tous fes travers. Cependant on le voit fondateur
" d'ordre, legiflateur de loix, qui vont de pair
" avec celles des Bafiles et des Pacomes; favant
" theologien, qui a fouvent pris la plume pour
" défendre les vérités orthodoxes attaquées de fon
" tems ; un grand maitre qui a formé de faints
" prélats, dont les lumieres ont long tems éclairé
" l'églife, qu'il a lui même enrichie de favans
" écrits, dont nous avons encore la meilleure partie.
" Mais la plus rare de toutes ces grandes qualités
" eft, qu'avec ce génie qui lui acquit une reputation
" des plus étendues, il eut la modeflie et l'humilité
" du plus parfait religieux. —L'enchaînement des
" matieres, qui ne permet pas d'écrire la vie
" d'Abeillard fans tracer en même tems celle
" d'Héloife, découvre le triomphe de la grace
" fur un cœur le plus attaché à la créature. Sa
" pénitence eft un exemple pour celles qui ont

" eu le malheur de l'avoir fuivie dans fa chute.
" Pendant vingt deux années qu'elle a furvecu
" à fon époux, elle eft un modele des vertus
" religieufes et de conduite pour les fuperieures.
" Enfin Héloife nous donne à douter fi la vie
" d'Abeillard eft plus digne de nos admirations
" que la fienne[a]."

After this opening, which is in the true ftyle
of panegyric, I was not to expect much truth of
character: for Abeillard, I was well aware, had
more in his compofition of the finner than the
faint, and in Heloifa the triumphs of grace were
not always fo brilliant as thofe of nature. No views
can be more oppofite than thofe of Bayle and Gervaife; but unhappily truth never lies in the ex-
tremes. Their portraits are fancy-pieces, which
may ferve to delineate the minds of the artifts, rather than the originals they are faid to reprefent.
I have, however, derived fome advantage from
Gervaife, and in general I have followed his arrangement of materials. The objects we view
very differently, and confequently our works have

[a] Pref. p. 3.

but a faint refemblance. Whofe eye be moſt juſt,
the reader may determine. I can fay, that I neglected nothing to clear the medium, and to fix a
proper point of view.

I alfo procured extracts from the *Annals* of Ar-
gentré and Papire Maſſon, from the *Hiſtory of
Britany* by Lobineau, and from Paſquier's *Refearches*. With thefe materials, joined to the information which the writers of the age fupplied, I
found myfelf in poffeffion of all the evidence, which
my fubject feemed to require. As far then as any
hiſtory can be pronounced genuine, the work I
prefent to the public may, I flatter myfelf, be
deemed fo.

It has been thought by fome that, I have chofen
a fubject which did not merit fo much attention.—
To the obfervation I know not what to reply: let
the work make its own apology. It was at leaſt
benevolent in me to wifh to free from obloquy two
characters, that had been much afperfed; and the
public, I think, fhould be pleafed with a narration,
which brings to their better acquaintance names,
which fo long were familiar to their ears. In

common life the incident is particularly agreeable. After all, what are the important matters which may be fuppofed to *merit* the refearches of the learned, and the notice of the public? I am not difpofed to think lightly of my contemporaries, or of their tafles and purfuits; but, I truft, the hiftory of Abeillard and Heloifa will not in all company, even the moft popular, fee reafon to blufh. I fpeak of the fubject only.

A few years ago, I remember, the *Memoirs* of Petrarch were in every body's hands, and the general intereft they excited was great. Shall I detract from the reputation of the Italian poet if I fay that Abeillard was as great a man as he? As great a poet he was not; nor was he employed, as Petrarch was, in the concerns of politics and the intrigues of courts. Fortune was more favorable to the Italian; but her beft gifts, the plaudits of admiring cities, and the fmiles of popes and potentates, could not make him happy, or fettle the eternal reftleff- nefs of his mind. Abeillard was equally admired by his contemporaries; his fame even had a wider fpread: but the oppofition of powerful enemies thwarted all his profpects, and dafhed his life with bitternefs. They were both lovers: and here as Abeillard was more fuccefsful, fo was his affection, while it lafted, more within the bounds of common fenfe and reafon. They both celebrated their miftreffes. At the time, the compofitions of Abeillard were in great vogue, and they were repeated in the politeft circles of Europe. Thofe of Petrarch have come down the ftream of time, buoyant, and fwelled by the gale of popular applaufe. Refufe our admiration to the various beauties they contain we cannot; but we may be permitted to think that Petrarch, when he praifed his Laura, was too precife and ingenious to be fincere. He wrote three hundred and eighteen fonnets in her praife, and eighty-eight fongs.

With more confidence Heloifa may enter the lifts with Laura. The latter (a little beauty only excepted, and to that the poet's pencil feems to have given no light tinge of coloring), poffeffed few endowments of art or nature. Virtuous fhe was and amiable; but we know fhe could not write, and we do not know that fhe could read. Heloifa, on the contrary, we may prefume, had equal beauty; and fhe had every qualification, which

nature, in her kindeſt humors, could give, or
education could perfeċt. I will not anticipate: but
ſhe was gentle and mild as innocence; learned as
the moſt learned of the age; her ſoul was Roman;
and her heart was a heart of fire.— Had Abeillard
and Heloiſa been bleſſed with a de Sade to colleċt
their *Memoirs*, with family-kindneſs, as Petrarch
and Laura have, they might have acquired,
perhaps, an equal ſhare of public notice and
eſteem.— In his treatiſe *de vita Solitaria*, Petrarch
ſpeaks of Abeillard, of his abilities, of ſome
events of his life, and of his misfortunes [1].

But though I may view in a favorable light the
two leading charaċters of my hiſtory, I was not leſs
ſenſible, that, auxiliary force would be neceſſary to
give them conſiſtency and due weight, in the public eye: I have therefore called to my aſſiſtance all
the great faċts and the principal perſonages, who
filled the period of the eighty-four years, which
meaſured the lives of Abeillard and Heloiſa. The
authors, I conſulted on theſe matters, are not numerous; for I was perſuaded that, to write with

[1] Lib. 2.

accuracy, it was better not to heap together many
volumes, which, if they did not perplex the judgement, could only ferve the oftentatious purpofe of
crowding the line of references with the difplay of
great names. — In ecclefiaftical hiftory, my chief
guides were Fleury and Natalis Alexander, in the
hiftory of France, Daniel: and in that of England,
Mr. Hume. Where I could, I alfo confulted the
original fources themfelves.

It is not, I am fure, neceffary that I fhould fay,
how good a man, and how great a hiftorian, abbé
Fleury was. Among his many valuable works, his
Hiftory of the Church, from its foundation to the
council of Conftance, ftands foremoft. It is rather
indeed a learned compilation, than a regular and
connected narration; but it contains every thing
which, the moft fcrupulous inquirer can wifh to
look for, and it is told with fimplicity and honeft
candor, which, at once portrays the amiable character of the writer, and delights the reader;
while he fays that, fuch muft be the man, whom
Truth would chufe for her hiftorian! —The preliminary *difcourfes* or differtations, interfperfed in
thefe volumes, are of infinite value. They are

written with more elegance and more care than the
general body of the hiſtory; and they treat of the
manner of writing hiſtory, of the eſtabliſhment of
chriſtianity, and of the various revolutions, which
have attended its progreſs, of the cruſades, of the
diſſenſions betwixt the church and the civil power, and of the origin and decline of religious orders.
On theſe ſubjects; ſo important and ſo delicate,
Fleury has ſaid all, that good ſenſe and the moſt
conſummate wiſdom could ſuggeſt, and he has ſaid
it with a freedom, which would do honor to
the moſt unprejudiced and philoſophic mind.
Without fear he brings to view the evils and groſs
abuſes which have disfigured the chriſtian eſtabliſhment; for he lays it down as a maxim, that all
truth ſhould be ſpoken; and with ſagacity he ſug-
geſts the remedies which ſhould be applied.—With
Fleury then I have made very free, and the reader
will thank me for it.

Natalis Alexander, or Alexander Noel, is another
French hiſtorian, whom I often quote. He wrote
very voluminouſly on eccleſiaſtical matters, and his
reſearches are profound and learned. The differtations, which are numerous, are calculated to

throw light on the dark and difficult points of hiftory. His quotations, from ancient authors, are full and accurate, which renders his compilation itfelf a library.—I have likewife had recourfe 'to Platina and Maimbourg, principally for the hiftory of the popes and the crufades.

Thefe I have mentioned are Roman Chatholic hiftorians; and it will be afked, if I have relied implicitly on their reprefentations?— Let it be obferved that, I am defcribing times which preceded the exiftence of Proteftantifm four hundred years; the *fources* of my information therefore muft neceffarily be catholic. As to modern writers, I chofe thofe, in whom, it feemed, I could place moft confidence; nor did I once think what mode of religion they had profeffed. But it will not among the learned, I fancy, as yet be made a queftion, which church has had the beft hiftorians.

Daniel, a dry and uninterefting narrator, I read for the hiftory of France, and Hume, fometimes, for that of England.

Thus I have mentioned my principal authors, and acknowledged my obligations. It remains that I fay, into what·arrangement I have thrown my

materials.—The whole period comprifes eighty-four
years, which I have divided into fuch portions, as
feemed beft adapted to mark the epochs of Abeillard's life ; and concomitant events and characters
of Europe I introduced, in their moft natural and
obvious order. I wifhed, as far as I was able, to
give every thing its proper place. The laft period
is much longer than the reft; but the reader will
fee, from the dearth of matter I labored under in
regard to the life of Heloifa, that it could not otherwife be difpofed.

Before I began my work, I wrote, in the moft
polite manner, to the abbefs of the Paraclet, requefting if fhe had any materials, which hitherto
had not feen the light, that fhe would favor me
with them; and at the fame time, I offered, with
as much gallantry as I thought was due to a venerable abbefs, to dedicate the work to her Ladyfhip.
She has taken no notice of my letter. Probably fhe
thought I was a heretic, with whom it might be
impious to co-operate (for I omitted to mention
the circumftance of my orthodoxy); or, which is
moft likely , fhe did not wifh her name fhould
appear at the head of a work, which, fhe might

think, would be rather a romance, than a ferious
hiftory. However, I can affure the reader, that
the abbey of the Paraclet poffeffes no records, of
the leaft moment, which have not, long ago, been
before the public. Amboife, he has feen, rummaged
every fhelf of their library.

I have fubjoined a tranflation of the celebrated
letters, with the originals themfelves, as given by
Amboife & Gervalfe. An edition of them was
publifhed in England, fome years ago, which I
have not feen. In other countries of Europe, as
in this, various fuppofed tranflations of the letters
have been circulated, which the gay and idle may
have read with pleafure; but they bear no refemblance to the original. They are the effufions of
fancy, and not defigned either to delineate the
charaflers of the lovers, or to promote the caufe of
virtue. It was fuch a tranflation, I believe, which
Mr. Pope had feen. His poem, with fear and
trembling, I have dared gently to criticize. As
to my own tranflation I feel for it no parental
fondnefs: it gives, I hope, the fenfe of the authors;
and to that only I pretend. I do not poffefs that
toiling and patient fteadinefs, which conflitutes

a good tranſlator.—Some paſſages I have curtailed,
and omitted others: the Latin, which is entire,
will ſuggeſt the motive.

My work I now ſubmit to the public with all
its imperfections. Where it merits praiſe, it will
find it ; and where it ſhould be cenſured, let cenſure freely fall. I know not what right the productions of the pen have to plead an exemption
from blemiſhes, to which the faireſt forms of nature are ſometimes liable : but as candor will
view theſe with indulgence, ſo will it the former.
Wilfully I have not meant to bring a ſlovenly and
unformed work before the public; and its unavoidable defects muſt be forgiven.

My hiſtory breaks off at a moſt brilliant and
important epoch. It is, when Henry Plantagenet
had juſt mounted the throne of England, when
his diſſenſions were ſoon to begin with Becket,
when Frederick Barbaroſſa was in Germany, when
Alexander III. was at Rome, and when the general aſpect of Europe ſeemed to promiſe events,
great and intereſting. The period has already
been ably treated; but ſhould the public favor
encourage me, *perhaps* I may be tempted again to

review it, though a noble lord, narrative from age
and unfair from prejudice, may be thought to
have exhaufted the fubject. A Roman Catholic
writer, attached to his religion, but unfhackled
in his thoughts, and free in his expreffions, is,
in this country, rather a new character in the
republic of letters. My abilities, alas! cannot
keep pace with my wifhes.

Ofcott, *near Birmingham*,
December 31, 1786.

THE

THE

INTRODUCTION.

IT has often been objected to hiftorians, that;
whatever period of ancient or of modern times
they might chufe to defcribe, they generally enter
on the fubject with a bias of ftrong prepoffeffion
on their minds. Certain characters they will be
fure to delineate, with too partial a fondnefs ;
while others will not have the common praife to
which they may juftly pretend. Alike unfair will
be their furvey of manners, events, opinions,
conduct. I believe, there is too much truth in the
charge. In revolving even the tranfactions of diftant
times, the mind is never abftracted from its own
peculiar inclinations. Thefe are followed in the
firft felection of the fubject, and their influence
does not afterwards ceafe. Naturally we admire
thofe characters, which may feem in fomething
to harmonize with our own, or which education,
and habits of thought, may have taught us to
admire. National difpofitions alfo, and religious

preventions, and fyftems of policy, come in aid
of the leading motives, and give, befides, a determined caft to the general view. The hiftorian fees
with his own eyes, and feels, in every defcription,
the emotions which are analogous to the temper
of his foul.

It fhould feem, however, in defcribing the
times which I have chofen, that there can be
nothing fufficiently interefting to excite this undue
predilection. The feelings of the reader are feldom
thofe of the writer. I have chofen, indeed, the
dark ages, thofe times, which it has long been
the fafhion to depreciate; over which ignorance
is thought to have fpread the dark mantle of
barbarifm and fuperftition, under which few traces
can be found which the improved and enlightened
minds of thefe days can furvey undifgufled. The
judgment is unequitable. I will not fay that there
was not much darknefs; but alfo there were many
rays, difperfed on characters, and beaming from
events, which the lefs faftidious hiftorian can collect
and view with pleafure. The darknefs was the
neceffary effect of caufes which, in every circumftance, were organized to produce it.

View of the
eleventh cen-
tury.
The Goths, the Huns, the Vandals, the Franks,
the Burgundians, and the Lombards, had defcended, like clouds of locufts, from the north,
and proudly fixed their iron thrones on the ruins
of the weftern world. Triumphant in their

ſtrength, they deſpiſed the puny nations they
had eaſily ſubdued. Arms and the animating ſports
of the field could alone gain their attention. To
them the arts were an unmanly occupation, and
as they knew nothing of ſcience, it even ſank lower
in their eſtimation. The manners and taſte of
the ruling party are ſoon communicated to the
other orders of ſociety. Theſe even will deſert
every former purſuit, and throw off the character
they before eſteemed, the better to conciliate the
favor, and to make their way to the notice, of
their new maſters. Thus did the people, whom
the barbarians had conquered, ſoon themſelves
become barbarous; the purſuits of ſcience languiſhed; and the powers of reaſon, for a time
difuſed, ſeemed to have loſt their native energy.

But as this diſpoſition of things, from the
natural inſtability of man, could not long continue, ſo did ſcience ſoon revive, and the arts
of peace were cultivated. Indeed, even in the
worſt moments, they were not utterly extin-
guiſhed, as we know from the annals of the
times. But in ſpeaking of events, a general view
only can be exhibited. I ſaid that ſcience ſoon
revived, and with it the arts. In their revival
they are but little ſuperior to the imperfection
of their firſt growth; languid, tardy, and element-
ary. Even in the eleventh century, the period
I have choſen, when the new kingdoms were

firmly eſtabliſhed, the view of ſociety is often uninviting, and ſometimes diſguſting from its barbarous and unenlightened character. But perhaps too ſevere a prepoſſeſſion had engaged the judgement. When I conſider the enlarged minds and the virtuous endowments of ſome men, who then lived, I am inclined to think it. The reader will determine.

About the fifteenth century, when the more elegant productions of antiquity began to be more generally read, to decry the monkiſh writers was deemed a proof of great diſcernment. Their language, indeed, was barbarous, compared with better models; but I would rather read a monkiſh compoſition, of which at leaſt the ideas are ſometimes original, than the works of thoſe faſtidious critics. Affectedly imitative of Ciceronean elegance, they are vapid and diſguſting. But we ourſelves have been led away by the puerile judgment of the men, I allude to. We do not ſufficiently reflect that, in the dark ages, even the moſt cultivated mind muſt have wanted language with which to clothe his ideas. Latin had long ceaſed to be ſpoken, and the modern tongues of Europe were as yet barren and unexpreſſive. They wrote in Latin. What judgment, let me aſk, would poſterity form of the claſſical elegance, at leaſt, even of theſe times, if modern authors were tied down to the uſe only of the dead languages? I know not that the editor of Bellendenus, whom some admire, could promise to himself a never-fading wreath of glory. Yet for these four hundred years, have the ages which preceded them been principally despised, because the language of their authors was rude and unharmonious.

Another circumstance has contributed to strengthen the unfavorable impression. When the Reformation began, in the sixteenth century, it was thought necessary to justify the measure by every plausible pretext. It was owing to the darkness in which the world had been involved, they said, that error had so successfully made its way, and had sapped the foundations of religious truth. In all their writings the first reformers dwell on this idea. The more gloomy the representation can be made, the more expedient becomes their work, and the greater success would attend their endeavours. Success did attend them; and their successors in the ministry have not been less sedulous to keep alive the same impression on the minds of the people. There was truth in the general view; but the deep coloring seemed sometimes to disguise its strongest features.

I mean not to write the apology of the dark ages; but I will take a short survey of the eleventh century, which may serve to introduce my reader to the period I have described in the following history.

c 3

Now was the Greek completely fevered from the
Latin church, by the induftry and bold perfeverance of Michael Cerularius, patriarch of Conftantinople. Photius, in the ninth century, had begun
the fchifm, a man of talents and of vaft learning,
but ambitious in defign, adulatory in addrefs, and
intemperate in every projeCL Michael was difpofed to accomplifh the work which his predecellor,
whofe memory he revered, had opened, and he
had abilities for it. Long had the patriarchs of
Conftantinople arrogated to themfelves the fplendid title of *univerfal bifhop*, a pretenfion which the
Roman pontiffs had ftrenuoufly oppofed. The underftanding between the two churches had feldom
been cordial. There were always fufficient fubjeCts to create jealoufies and animofity. They now
broke out with unufual rancor. The eaftern
patriarch brought forward his charges againft the
Latin church. They were trivial, and could not
juftify the divifion he projeCled; but the effeCl anfwered his moft fanguine hopes. His accufations
were, that the Latins in their facrifice ufed unlea-
vened bread; that they ate of ftrangled meats;
that they did not fing alleluia in Lent; and that
fometimes they fafted on Saturdays. Such charges
hardly merited a ferious reply. The pope,
however, Leo IX, was irritated; and the intemperance of his conduCt, which his minifters did

but aggravate, gave an air of equity to meafures which were affumed in levity and ambition. To overthrow moft effectually the extravagant preten-fions of Cerularius, Leo dares to produce his own: "Know," fays he, "that my fovereignty "reaches to heaven, and extends over all the king-"doms of the earth." The Greek was not convinced; and from that moment the fatal fchifm was figned, which no efforts have been fince able to repair[1].

The wealth of the church had, through a long Weftern fucceffion of years, been increafing, and with it church the temporal power and influence of its minifters. They were poffeffed of domains and principalities. The two jurifdictions, which in their own natures are effentially diftinct, became thus confounded, and the paftor of the flock was the lord of the people. Rome, from the days of Conftantine, had grown rich and powerful. The piety of fome, the liberality of others, and the miftaken zeal of more, had continually added to its poffeffions. But from the moment it became cuftomary for the pope to crown the weftern emperor, the prerogatives of his fee arofe to an immeafurable magnitude. He that could give a diadem, it was faid, poffeffed a power above him who bowed his head to receive it. The princes themfelves, whofe intereft it often was, contributed by their fubmiffion to ftrengthen

[1] Fleury, &c.

the illufion. It was, in this century, as will be feen, that the power of Rome was in its greateft altitude.

Accuftomed to view Europe in its prefent ftate, when general intereft, in fpite of political diffenfions, is made a bond of union, the retrofpeck into times when nations ftood alone, is cold and uninterefting. I can therefore look to Rome, with real fatisfaction, when with propriety it might be called the centre of civil union. It connected kingdoms, it fwayed their interefts, it controuled the abufe of power, it received appeals from the oppreffed, it awed the vicious, it diftributed juftice, it ftrengthened and gave rewards to virtue.

The popes of this century (I mean as far as Gregory VII.) were not men of great abilities or of great virtues. I muft except Leo IX. and Alexander II. The firft of thefe had high endowments. Inceffantly he labored to reform the vices of the church; he affembled councils, and he oppofed the fpreading torrent of fimony and incontinence. He travelled much, ftriving every where to re-eftablifh difcipline, and to correct abufes. To the fervor of his zeal correfponded the innocence of his own life. He was the father of the poor, and the refuge of the miferable, and he spent his days in penitence, prayer, and good works. This was the fair side of Leo. In his conduct towards the patriarch of Constantinople and his abettors, he was less mild, less forbearing, and less prudent. But when a party of Norman marauders had entered Italy, and plundered his territories, the pontiff would not brook the daring insult. He collected an army, and marched at their head. In a pitched battle his forces were defeated, and himself was taken prisoner. The conquerors treated the venerable captive with the greatest respect ; but they detained him. He died in their hands [*]. — The courtly annalist, Baronius, is offended that this action of Leo should have been censured as contrary to christian meekness , and he justifies it by the allegory of the two swords.

It is remarkable that Leo, in his letter to Cerularius, which I mentioned, reproaches the Greeks with having raised a woman to the patriarchate of Constantinople. This he would not have done, had the adventures of pope Joan been then known. Modern sagacity, however, has discovered that the event happened in the ninth century, near two hundred years before Leo.

Benedict VIII. had also exhibited a spirit, equally martial and magnanimous. The Saracens landed

[*] Baron. Annal. ad an. 1053.

in Tuſcany, and puſhing on their conqueſts,
threatened the gates of Rome. The pontiff aſſembled his biſhops and the champions of the church,
when it was reſolved inſtantly to attack the enemy.
The pope marched. At the ſame time a fleet was
ordered to be out at ſea to intercept their retreat.
The infidels were routed, and not a man is
ſaid to have eſcaped the ſword. The prince of
the Saracens, whom this overthrow of his people
had exaſperated, and whoſe queen had loſt her
head by the pontiff's order, ſent to Benedict
a ſack full of cheſnuts, ſignifying by his meſſenger, that, the next ſpring, he would land
as many ſoldiers, on the ſhores of Italy. " Take,"
ſaid the pope, " this purſe of millet back to
" your maſter; it will tell him the number of
" my brave men who ſhall meet him at his
" landing'."   ı

My motive in relating theſe anecdotes is to
ſhow, what was the ſpirit of the age; and to
ſuggeſt the reflection, that, even virtuous characters are ſometimes compoſed of very extraordinary materials.

As the tiara was become an object of more
ambition, than the imperial crown, it was often
ſought for by men, whom the luſt of power
only inſtigated to mount the ſacred chair.
Factions were formed to ſupport the candidates.
Thus, in 1033, was elected Benedict IX, a youth

<hr>

' Baron. Annal.

of twelve years, who difgraced the holy office by a life of infamy *. — Without the miraculous intervention of providence the evil was inevitable. Good men lamented it ; but they feemed not fufficiently to know what the means were which could alone prevent its repetition. They fhould have divefled the holy fee of that power and external pageantry , which were its irrefiftible allurements. In the brighteft ages of the church, the popes of Rome were the paflors only of the people. The days are returning to us.

I find , at this time, in the church of Europe, many learned and virtuous bifhops. While war, with its concomitant evils , diflurbed the peace of fociety, to their courts retired the ftudious and gentle-minded, and they found protection in them. They cultivated the fciences , imperfect as they were , and they tutored the youth to virtue. Their piety, though not always enlightened, was fincere, and to the duties of religion they dedicated their lives. From the nature of the feudal compact, which now prevailed, the bifhops were bound to martial fervice. Many ferved in perfon ; fuch was the character of the age : while others were fatisfied to fend their contingent of men and horfes, at the fummons of their lord. A bifhop, accoutred for the field , and marching at the head of his vaffals, was no uncommon fight. The frowning helmet , he thought, became him better, than the gairifh

* Baron. An.

mitre. Fatal to the fpirit of ecclefiaflical difcipline was this propoflcrous arrangement [1].

Many new convents were now formed, and difcipline was reftored to others. They alfo became afylums to fcience and to virtue. The piety and fervent zeal of the firft ages feemed to revive. The effect was generally felt, and the profligacy of the times was powerfully counteracted [2]. —I wifh the reader to be fenfible that to many objects there is a fair and a foul fide. If I dwell with moft pleafure on the firft, is my tafte reprehenfible? But to this tafte, I would not facrifice the fmalleft element of truth.

Political ftate of Europe. In the political world there is much to furvey, could my limits allow it.—Henry, the Second of the name, was Emperor in Germany. The hiftorians of the age are lavifh in his praifes; for never had the church a better friend. He was a father alfo to his people, and his patriotifm and martial prowefs were as celebrated as his piety. His devotion to the holy fee was unbounded. With Cunegundis, his queen, he went to Rome, where from the hand of Benedict VIII. they received the imperial crown. Baronius remarks that, no one was then called Emperor, who had not fubmitted to this ceremony. It was thus performed. Henry, furrounded by twelve Roman fenators, of whom fix were fhaved, and

[1] Fleury, difc. 3.   [2] Ibid.

fix wore long beards, with flaves in their hands,
proceeded to the church of St. Peter. Cunegundis
was by his fide. The pope waited in the porch.
He here afked the king, if he would ever defend
the Roman fee, and bear true allegiance to himfelf and fucceffors. Henry bowed affent. They
were then introduced; both were anointed, and
both received a crown from the hand of the pontiff. The fame day they fupped with Benedict in
the Lateran palace '. — Henry then, by an ample
diploma, confirmed to the Roman fee all its ancient privileges, and the donations which his predeceffors had made of the fovereignty of Rome and
the exarchate of Ravenna.

The weftern empire, which had been extinguifh-
ed in Auguftulus, was reflored in the ninth century,
in the perfon of Charlemagne, king of France,
who extended his conquefts into part of Spain,
and into Italy, and Flanders, and Germany, and
part of Hungary. The imperial crown continued
in the different branches of his family. But as the
emperors, to indulge their favorites, or compelled
by circumftances, had erected many petty fovereigns
in their ftates, thefe grew powerful; and on the
death of Lewis IV. in 910, they declared that
the imperial dignity had devolved on the Germanic
body. Conrad, duke of Franconia, was therefore

' Ditm. In Baron.

elected emperor, to whom fucceeded Henry F.
duke of Saxony, the anceflor of the Henry, I
have mentioned. His fucceffor was Conrad II.

St. Stephen, the firft king of Hungary, and its
apoftle, is another. prince, with whofe praifes the
hiftories of the age refound. And, as far as we can
judge, he was deferving of them. Early in his
reign, when he was but duke of Hungary, he fent
an ambaffador to Rome to procure 'from his
holinefs the confirmation of the pious foundations
he had made, and of the bifhoprics he had erected;
and, at the fame time, to requeft that he would
confer on him the title of king. The pope approved of all his meafures, and prefented him with
a rich crown, which had been defigned for the
brows of Miceflas, duke of Poland. The motives
for this preference were cogent. Stephen, by his
ambaffador, had fubmitted his kingdom to the
protection of the holy fee '.

Having converted his people to chriftianity, and
civilized their barbarous manners, his next care
was to make them happy. He eftablifhed an
excellent code, which, at this day, is the bafis of
the laws of Hungary, and he attended to their
execution. He was a faint and a legiflator. He
was alfo a warrior; and the fuccefs of his arms
correfponded with the equity of his caufe. Under
him Hungary became a great and flourifhing

' Baron.

nation, and his memory is ftill held in the warmeft veneration, by that brave and independent people.

In France reigned Robert, and after him Henry I. his fon. Robert was an amiable, a beneficent, a pious, and a learned prince. He had married Birtha, his coufin, which drew on him the fevereft cenfures of the church. While under the fentence of excommunication, two fervants only were permitted to approach his perfon; and as every thing which he touched was polluted, they were careful to burn, or to pafs through a flame, the cups and difhes which were ufed at his table. To this tho' king fubmitted; but he would not furrender his wife. In the mean time, Birtha was delivered of a child, with the head and neck of a goofe, fays a contemporary writer[*]. Robert relinquifhed her, and married Çonftance of Arles, a turbulent and headftrong woman.

From an interview between himfelf and the Emperor Henry, we may collect the difinterefled and pious fpirit of the age. They met on the banks of the Mofelle. After the bufinefs of the congrefs had been amicably adjufted, Robert prefented his imperial friend with a hundred horfes richly caparifoned, each carrying a complete fuit of armour and a helmet. Thefe Henry refufed

[*] Pet. Damis.

But from among other magnificent gifts, which lay before him, he chofe a book of the gofpels, highly ornamented, and a cafket containing the tooth of St. Vincent. Robert, the next day, fhowed an equal difintereftednefs. From a hundred weight of pure gold he took only a pair of ear-rings, which were then worn by men, or as fome tranflate it, two veffels for his table". — He is faid to have been the firft king of France who touched for the *evil*.

In the reign of the next prince, an expert warrior and a prudent ftatefman, we read of little elfe but diffenfions and battles. Then began the violent contefts between the crown and the dukedom of Normandy. Robert, the fecond of the name, with a holy enthufiafm, departing for Jerufalem, left his dominions to his natural fon, William, a youth of nine years. The little hero was oppofed by his own vaffals, and the king, with many powerful princes, foon combined againft him. He triumphed over them, learning in the field and in the cabinet, the maxims of policy and the energy of action, which in a few years would exalt him to the Englifh throne.

Of England, during this period, the hiftory is well known. It comprifes the reign of Ethelred, with the melancholy recital of the Danifh incurfions, and the final fubmiffion of the country to

---

¹° Glaber, apud Baron.

the

the invaders. Then reigned Canute, a great and wife monarch; and Harold and Hardicanute, his fons, for nothing commendable, but for agility and ftrength of body. In Edward, the confeffor, who fucceeded, we again find a prince, whom hiftorians have praifed without meafure. He was humane, juft, and pious, and his people loved him; but he wanted vigor and capacity. The profperity of his reign owed lefs to his abilities, than to the conjunctures of the times. His want of children proved fatal to the Saxon line.

At what other time, in the annals of Europe, fhall we find fuch a knot of kings as thefe? But while they were laboring to extend juftice, or to humanize their people, or to propagate, what they conceived to be, the beft maxims of religion and truth, a new kingdom was forming on the Italian fhore. Tancred, a noble Norman, lord of Hauteville, with his twelve fons, and a gallant army of adventurers, left their country, in 1008, and landing in Apulia, foon expelled the Saracens, and the Greeks their confederates. Succefs attended their future operations, though cruelty and injuftice too often marked their progrefs. From this time the Normans became dukes of Calabria, and counts and dukes of Apulia. Robert Guifcard, the boldeft Norman of them all, augmented his power by the conqueft of Sicily, Naples, and all the lands which lie between that city and the territory of

Rome. Roger, his fon, was faluted by the pope, king of both the Sicilies ".

Robert Guifcard had given his daughter, Helena, in marriage to Conftantine, fon of Michael Ducas, emperor of Conftantinople. Michael being dethroned by Nicephorus, his fon and daughter were caft into prifon. The infult roufed the Norman hero, and he marched towards the eaft at the head of fifteen thoufand men. In the mean time, Alexius Comnènus had ufurped the imperial throne. Guifcard continued his march, when in Albania he was met by Alexius. The imperial army was a hundred and fifty thoufand ftrong. Robert viewed the mighty hoft, and prepared for battle. On his knees he fpent two watches of the night with his army, and with the rifing fun attacked the enemy. They were routed, and fled in confufion. Succefs attended his other operations, and he fixed his eye on the throne of Conftantinople. But difturbances in the weft called him away to fupport his friend, Gregory VII. againft the attacks of the German Henry.

The hiftory of Spain, at this time, is too complicated and too romantic, to afford matter for ferious difcuffion. The authors are many, but their violent attachment to the Spanifh caufe, and their hatred to the Moors, had rendered them blind to impartial truth. Yet, abftracting from

" Baron.

religion, we well know on which fide lay fcience, and the arts which can ennoble and embellifh human nature.

As to the writers of the age, in general, I know not what to fay. Their compofitions, as far as may be concluded from extracts, are not always inelegant; nor are they void of accuracy, in hiftorical narration. Their commentaries on fcripture, and their controverfial writings, only that they point out the religious tenets of the time, have little merit, to us at leaft, who can recur to better models. But it is the credulity of their beft writers, ever dwelling on miracles and legendary tales, which gives furprife. On other occafions they feem to have been men, not void of judgment and perfpicuous fenfe. It is a problem not eafy to be folved. Could we tranfport ourfelves back to their times, and feize the affociation of ideas which had occupied their minds, we might difcover how they faw and reafoned. It was the natural effect of circumftances, which then no fuperior fenfe or better organization could have furmounted. Man is a part of the general fyftem which time rolls on, and is fubject to its laws. They were as wife as they could be; and if we are wifer, it is, becaufe a new order of things has rifen to our view. The time will arrive, when this age alfo may be denominated dark; and who knows, but they may fay, we were *credulous ?* Our anceftors, I doubt not, thought themfelves as little under the influence of prejudice and idle fancy, as we may deem ourfelves; and to fpeak equitably, agreeably to the idea I fuggefted, can it be faid, that they were deceived?

The ordeal-trials, by boiling water, or red-hot iron, were now in great ufe. In vain had councils by their canons, and popes by their decrees, attempted to fupprefs them. The fuperflitious obftinacy of the age could not be controuled. Yet if we can at all rely on accounts, which come down to us with all the air of authenticity, it muft be owned that the event of thefe trials was fometimes truly wonderful. In 1067, were great diffenfions in Florence between the bifhop and the people. They acoufed him of having obtained their fee by fimoniacal practices. The monks of a neighbouring convent fupported the accufation. The bifhop denied the charge. In this ftate of indecifion, which no ordinary procefs could then terminate, the monks offered to verify their accufation by the trial of fire. The bold challenge was applauded by the people, and they affembled round the convent. Two piles of wood were raifed, ten feet long, five feet wide, and four feet high. A fpace of fix feet feparated the piles, which was alfo covered with combuftible materials. A young monk, named Peter, came forward.

He had been chofen for the awful ceremony, and
he was habited in his prieftly veftments. By order
of his abbot he then advanced to the altar, and
began the fervice of the day. The people, filent
and in dread expectation, waited round the altar.
Towards the clofe of the facrifice, four monks
came down to fet fire to the piles. They carried
in their hands twelve lighted torches. In an inftant
the piles were in a blaze. Peter, having finifhed
the fervice, advanced towards the fires, bearing
a crofs in his hand, and finging with the choir
as he advanced. Silence being made, the conditions
of the trial were read to the people. They applauded with loud acclamations, and called on heaven
to fupport its own caufe.

By this time the piles were nearly reduced to
glowing embers; when Peter, ftanding at a fmall
diftance, pronounced, with a firm voice, the following prayer : " Lord Jefus," faid he, " if Peter
" of Pavia has ufurped by fimony the fee of
" Florence, fuccour me, I befeech thee, in this
" tremendous trial, and fave me from this fire,
" as thou didft preferve the three children in the
" burning furnace." So faying he embraced his
brethren ; and the people were afked, how long
they chofe, he fhould remain in the fire? Let him
but pafs flowly through it, faid they.—He fixed
his eyes on the crofs, and with a gay countenance
flowly entered the burning paffage. His feet

were bare. For a time he was invisible in the
smoke; but he soon appeared, on the other side,
safe and uninjured. The flame seemed gently to
move his hair, and his linen garments floated
lightly on the current; but not even the hairs on
his legs were singed. The people crowded round
him; fell at his feet, and called him their deliverer
and the friend of heaven ". — The bishop confessed
his guilt and was deposed.

The account is abridged from the letter which
the clergy and people of Florence wrote to the
pope on the occasion; and its truth is attested by
the historians of the age. Peter was afterwards
made a cardinal and bishop of Albano. He acquired the name of *igneus.*

I could mention many similar events, but none
so splendid as this. Our philosophers, versed in
the chymistry of nature, will account for the
phenomenon. To me it seems, that heaven,
propitious to the good intentions and simplicity
of the age, might sometimes perhaps thus visibly
announce itself, to excite a just horror of crimes,
which by their frequency had ceased to be
regarded. I cannot, at least, subscribe to that
fastidious criticism, which rejects every fact as
fabulous, that does not square with the measure
of modern maxims and theories.

" Baron, Fleury.

The virtues of the eleventh century were valor
and devotion, (if the former can pretend to the
name,) and its vices were cruelty, superstition, and
intemperance. The transition from one to the
other is easy, and the alliance natural. Valor,
where education does not check its exuberance,
runs out to ferocity; and devotion, unallayed by
reason, is the parent of superstition. Intemperance
must be found, where, in a society not restrained
by the rules of decorum, the grosser passions have
the first claim to indulgence. But where valor
is, there will be a certain dignity of character,
supported by generosity, by honor, and a con-
tempt of what is base and mercenary. When
devotion mixes with valor, it causes an enthusiasm, which no dangers or difficulties can inti-
midate.

In many characters of the age I find these virtues, and near them might all the vices be likewise
found: they grew naturally from the soil. But the
reader has seen men, in whom was virtue unsullied
by any vice. On the throne he saw just and virtuous monarchs; in the field brave and generous
warriors ; in the church zealous and charitable
bishops; and in the common walks of life there
were men , emulous to copy the virtues they
admired in their superiors.

From the above sketch, the manners of the
people may be easily traced. Their valor would

be brutality ; and their devotion would be fuperftition. It is the natural gradation. In thofe
two features is portrayed the ftrong outline of the
eleventh century. — I faid, I did not mean to
apologize for its faults, or to blazon its virtues.
There is a temperate and tranquil medium
through which objects are feen in their true pro-
portions. Through that medium I ftrove to
direct my fight ; and if I have fucceeded, I have
prepared a proper *Introduction* to the following
hiftory:

C O N T E N T S

FIRST VOLUME.

---

*Abeillard's birth and education—He travels and comes
to Paris — State of learning — He studies under
Champeaux, and quarrels — Teaches at Melun and
Corbeil — Subjects in debate — He falls sick, and retires — Returns to Paris — Contends with de Champeaux and triumphs — Goes again into Britany —
Resolves to study theology— Gregory VII. pope —
State of France — State of England — The first
crusade.*　　　　　　　　　　　PAGE 1 — 70

BOOK II.

*Abeillard goes to Laon and studies under Anselm —
Returns to Paris and teaches. — Heloifa —Abeillard
becomes her master — She escapes with him into
Britany — He offers to marry her — They are mar-
ried — He conveys her to Argenteuil — Fulbert's
revenge — Pascal II. pope — France and England
—Religious orders — Cluni — The Chartreuse —
Fontevraud,*　　　　　　　　　PAGE 71 — 109

f

CONTENTS.

BOOK III.

BOOK IV.

THE

THE

HISTORY

OF THE LIVES OF

ABEILLARD and HELOISA.

BOOK I.

*His birth and education — He travels, and comes to
Paris — State of learning — He studies under Champeaux and quarrels — Teaches at Melun and Corbeil — Subjects in debate — He falls sick and retires — Returns to Paris — Contends with de Champeaux and triumphs — Goes again into Britany —
Resolves to study theology — Gregory VII. Pope. —
State of France — State of England — The first
crusade.*

Anno, 1079.

PETER ABEILLARD was born in the vil-
lage of Palais, four leagues from Nantes, in Little Britany, towards the close of the eleventh century,
in the year 1079 [1]. His father's name was Berenger,
a gentleman of noble descent, and Abeil lardis

' Hist. Calam.

thought to have been the eldest of many children. Berenger, before he entered the army, had been early instructed in the elements of such learning as the age had to supply, and he ever after retained ·a fondness for letters: he was careful therefore that, in the education of his children, whilst their bodies were formed to arms, the more excellent culture of their minds should not be neglected. The church or arms were then the only fashionable professions of gentlemen, and, with the addition of the law, the same continues to be the taste of all polite nations to the present day.

Abeillard came into the world with the happiest dispositions: his mind, gentle as the air of Britany, and fertile as its soil, was open to all the impressions of literary discipline. So he speaks of himself '. — Fable relates (for there was a time when the birth of every great man was attended by some marvellous circumstance) that his mother had sure forebodings of his future eloquence, and therefore from the bee, called him Abeillard: she saw honey falling from his lips '. — Being his father's favorite, his education was more sedulously guarded; and very soon such fast hold had the love of letters taken of his mind, that they became the ruling passion of his life. Destined to arms, he lost all relish for the pursuits of that

' Hist. Calam. ' Vie d'Abeil.

brilliant and feductive profeffion, and he refigned his inheritance, with all the rights of primogeniture, to his younger brothers. "At the feet "of Minerva, fays he, I facrificed all the mi-"litary pomp which blazes round the car of the "God of War *."

But what were the charms, which, at that gloomy period of fallen fcience, could have power to captivate the ardent mind of Abeillard? To judge from his writings, he was not unacquainted with the beft authors of the pureft age of Roman literature; them, under his father's eye, he had probably made his favorite purfuit; and thefe ftudies, as they had ornamented his mind, fo had they prepared him to enter on a new career, in which alone, at that time, the afpiring ambition of youth could meet an object ample enough to fatisfy its defires.

Philofophy, or more properly that branch of it, which is termed logic, or the art of difputation, was then rifing into renown; and that our young fcholar might have every advantage, which could be given him, of being thoroughly initiated into its various arts, he was put under the tuition of Rofcelin, the acuteft logician of the age '. —·Rofcelin, lefs fkilled in theology, than in the fubtilties of his art, brought himfelf, fome years

* Hift. Calam.   ' Præf. Apologet.

B 3

after, into great trouble, on account of the very
fingular notions he had introduced into the myfterious doctrine of the Trinity. He was a Tritheift.
For this he was condemned in the council of
Compiegne, 1092 [*].

Under fo able a mafter, Abeillard, it is not to be
doubted, made a rapid advance: the ftudy was
well adapted to his genius: acute and penetrating,
he would eagerly devote himfelf to inquiries,
which opened to his view an extenfive fcene, that
feemed to call all the powers of his foul into action,
and where he could promife to himfelf at once the
difplay of abilities, and the glory of conqueft.—The
victories of the fchools had then their charms, as
foothing perhaps to vanity as were thofe of the field,
and furely they were more innocent. The laurels,
indeed, which wreathed the brows of the literary
champion, were not, in the eye of the multitude,
fo awfully dignified, but they drew very general
admiration, nor were they fullied with a fingle
drop of human blood.

Having thus provided for the future reputation
of his fon, in a manner which feemed to enfure
his fuccefs, Berenger withdrew from the noify
fcene of arms, to the retirement of a convent. —
The cloifter was then the ufual retreat of men;
whom either difappointment had difgufted of the

[*] Fleury, vol. xiii.

world, or indolence rendered unfit for its active purfuits. It was likewife an afylum, to which religion or the gentle voice of humanity called many, who looked with horror on the enormities of a barbarous and warlike age. Kings were feen to refign their crowns for the monkifh cowl, and the walls of the convents thronged with inhabitants of all ages, and of every fex and condition. Abufes and great crimes were the neceffary confequence of this promifcuous affemblage of men: but, at the times I am defcribing, the worft exceffes of the cloiftered life were but puny evils when compared with the rapines, the murders, the extortions, which, with impunity, were practifed on the great theatre of the world.

From his cell, Berenger thought to view, in undifturbed repofe, the fplendid career of his fon Abeillard; nor were his expectations fruftrated. The young man had hardly reached his fixteenth year, but he felt himfelf fufficiently ftrong to rely on his own exertions, and he quitted his mafters, whofe inftructions, as he had little more to learn from them, could only retard the expanfion of his mind '. — When, by proper difcipline, the youthful character has been fometime habituated to the forms of order and of claffic rule, it fhould be left to itfelf; it will take its own bent, and profper beft.

He travels, and comes to Paris.

' Vie d'Abeil.

B 3

Britany could no longer fatisfy his wifhes; he withdrew therefore from his native country, and with an ardor, which fhowed the great defire he had of improvement, he rapidly ran over the neighbouring provinces, in queft of fcience [1]. —In this, he propofed to himfelf the example of thofe ancient philofophers, whofe lives he had read, and whom he thought it glorious to imitate. Over their minds the love of wifdom held an unbound-ed control. " I emulated, " fays he, the fame of the peripatetic fchool, and in whatever " quarter, I was told. the ftudy of philofophy " was purfued. thither I went, that no fources " of fcience might be hidden from me [1]. " —But when the provincial fchools had nothing more to give, Abeillard turned his eyes to Paris; where he arrived about the laft year of the eleventh century, and in the twentieth year of his age.

State of Learning. The fchools of Paris, for more than a century, had been rifing to a great reputation, and they were now become the general mart of fcience, to which reforted fcholars from all the kingdoms of Europe [20]. The circumftance of its being the principal refidence of the French monarchs contri-buted not a little to give it celebrity, and to draw to it the ableft mafters. — Since the revival of knowledge in the weftern empire, under the aufpicious eye of Charlemagne, in the eighth

[1] Hift. Cal.   [1] Ib.   [20] Fleury, Dupin, &c.

century, the greateft monarch perhaps that ever
fwayed the fceptre, and whom the warrior, the
man of letters, and the chriftian might call his
friend, the French nation had taken the lead in
the progrefs of the arts of literature. Yet when
compared with the rapid defcent, by which the
human mind, from the height of fcience and
polifhed life, is hurried into ignorance and barbarifm, how flow and almoft imperceptible is the
return it makes even to the firft dawnings of the
new day, which, in the revolutions of ftates and
kingdoms, is fometimes deftined to rife upon us!

Alcuin, the luminary of a dark age, whom Britain gave to Charlemagne to be his inftructer and
his guide, had traced out the lines, by which,
he thought, fcience might be the fooneft reftored.
Thefe rules had been carefully purfued, and
though they had led to no fplendid improvements,
yet the fault lay not fo much in the method, as
in the tardy conftitution of the human mind. He
had recommended to begin by orthography (a
neceffary preliminary, undoubtedly, when even
the Emperor himfelf was unable to write his own
name;) to this was to fucceed the ftudy of grammar, of rhetoric, and laftly of philofophy, in its
three branches, of logic, morals, and nature: but
logic, or what I have already more properly cal-

B 4

BOOK
I.

led, the art of difputation, was the only portion of that divine fcience, which was thought
worthy to engrofs the attention of literary ambition ".

The rules of grammar, which, in every country, fhould be primarily applied to its native
tongue, were then folely directed to the ftudy of
the Latin language; though Latin had ceafed to
be fpoken, and all the infant tongues of Europe
were in a ftate of the loweft barbarifm. Nor yet was
this privileged tongue itfelf raifed to any degree of
claffical perfection. So true is it, that the arts
and fciences, in their moft minute ramifications,
keep an exact pace with the ebbs and flows of
human nature. — Rhetoric they alfo ftudied;
but it was a rhetoric which taught them to depart
from the noble fimplicity of truth, and in its
ftead to fubftitute an affected jargon of language,
and a whimfical difplay of metaphorical figures.
The writings of Alcuin himfelf atteft the juftnefs
of thefe obfervations. — Nor was their famous
logic, which attracted the attention of the admiring
world, a jot more valuable. It was no longer, what
it had been, under its firft mafters, in the fchools
of Greece, the art of accurate reafoning, whereby
truth was difcovered, and its bounds enlarged, by

" Fleury, Dupin, &a.

an eafy procefs, an error was detected; but now it confifted in the mere exercife of difputation, in the fubtle arrangement of unmeaning terms, which clouded reafon, and enveloped truth. Applaufe and not inftruction was the object of the mafters; and he was the greateft adept who, by captious quibbles, could diftrefs his adverfary the moft ".

As the mind was thus bewildered in a maze of fophiftry, fo was the real fcience of man and of nature utterly neglected. They knew nothing of the mechanical powers of the world, and every uncommon appearance was confidered as a certain prefage of extraordinary events: they afcribed them to myftic or to moral caufes. — Their ethics ran out into idle fpeculations, into definitions and divifions of vice and virtue, whilft practical documents and the high duties of life were little regarded. — The important bufinefs of criticifm, to which modern times are indebted for all they poffefs, in the line of fcientific improvement, was equally unknown as the ways of nature. Fables they received as genuine facts, and the more extraordinary an event was, the greater was its claim to credibility ".

But fchools were opened, and monafteries were alfo founded, wherein inftruction was gratuitoufly diftributed, and the crowds of fcholars, who

" Fleury, Dupin, &c.   " Fleury, difc. 5.

attended, were numerous beyond belief. It feemed
as if the mind of man, tired out in the horrid
fcenes of bloodfhed, which had fo long difgraced the annals of Europe, were returning to juft-
er notions, and that a new order of things were
preparing to rife. And fo it was; but the great
event was as yet diftant, in the way to which lay
a long and dreary chafm of more than four hundred years.

Paris, I have faid, was the great centre of all
the knowledge which the eleventh century could
boaft of, and to this theatre I had conducted my
young philofopher. His heart, doubtlefs beat
with quicker pulfations, when he entered thofe
walls, which were foon to atteft his triumphs,
and which had long been the object of his ardent
wifhes.

He ftudies
under Cham-
peaux and
quarrels.
Among the mafters, whofe reputation was great
in the fchools, William de Champeaux was the
moft eminent. Contemporary writers fpeak highly of his abilities and of his virtues, and he was
deeply verfed, they tell us, and well exercifed
in all the arts of the dialectic difcipline [n]. As
with painful emulation he had rifen to the higheft
honors in his profeffion, fo was he jealous of
the fame he had acquired, and feared the moft
diftant rival. The leffons of this man Abeillard

[n] Quercet. Notae

frequented, and he was much pleafed with the choice he had made. His fluency of language and the acutenefs of his reafoning, feemed to throw new charms over his favorite art. In animation of fpirit, he foon began to fkirmifh with the foremoft of the fcholars, and fometimes he dared to queftion even de Champeaux himfelf ". The veteran was delighted with the prompt character of his difciple, and augured to himfelf a frefh increafe of fame from the exertion of abilities, which, he flattered himfelf, he fhould foon be able to draw out in the fupport of his own opinions.

In thefe difpofitions of mutual benevolence, from which the youthful mind of Abeillard pictured to itfelf fcenes of future happinefs, a commerce of friendfhip began, and he was taken to board into the houfe of his mafter. From this circumftance, as he had more frequent opportunities of improvement, fo might he foon learn that de Champeaux was not a hero at all times; and the blaze of glory which had feemed to furround him among the plaudits of his fcholars, infenfibly vanifhed when viewed with a familiar eye. He began to fufpect that this wide-fpreading tree was perhaps rather loaded with leaves than fruit. — The ftripling now walked with a bolder ftep into the fchools: he dared publicly to contend with

" Hift. Calam.

Champeaux; he attacked, in serious language
some even of his most favored opinions; he repeated these attacks daily with more petulance; and
sometimes, says he, I seemed to feel a superiority
in argument ". — The eye of the philosopher
looked benevolence no longer; confused, angry,
mortified, he left his seat; and Abeillard was
soon obliged to provide himself with another establishment.

Nor was it de Champeaux alone who felt this
galling humiliation: many of the first students, at
once envious of the growing fame of the young
Briton, and stung by the flippancy of his
retorts, under the disguise of supporting their master, thus wantonly attacked, were loud in their
indignation. But the general applause of the
public went with him; for he was young, handsome, witty, and agreeable ".

The schools, as we know from the histories of
the age, were not only filled with students, as at
present; but men in years, persons of distinction,
fathers of families, and ministers of state, after the
toils of the day were over, crowded to them as to a
theatre of amusement. There was novelty in the
scene, and Latin, the language of the disputants,
was very generally understood. The tournaments

" Hist. Calam.   " Præf. Apologet.

and other martial exercifes, which, foon after prevailed in Europe, were to the body, what thefe controverfies had been to the mind. The gauntlet of defiance was here alfo thrown down, and bold or prefumptuous was the man, who dared to take it up.

Abeillard, now cónfident from fuccefs, and elated by tlíe applaufe of his admirers, weighed his own powers, and thought them equal to any attempt. He was twenty-two years old; an age, when the human mind, in the fpringtide of paffion, views the labors of Hercules, as the eafy bufinefs of a morning's amufement. " I was "young indeed, fays he, but confident of myfelf, " my ambition had no bounds: I afpired to the " dignity of a profeffor, and only waited till I " could fix on a proper place to open my " lectures ""."

The court often refided at Melun, then a confiderable town on the Seine, ten leagues above Paris. The circumftance was highly favorable to his views, could he obtain permiffion to fettle there: but it was not eafily to be effected. The intereft of de Champeaux and his friends, he knew, was great, and all this intereft would be exerted to counteract his defigns. It is true; nothing was left unattempted againft him; fecret

"" Hift. Calam.

machinations and open oppofition were all in motion; but the good fortune of Abeillard prevailed. De Champeaux had fome enemies among the great; the refentful motives which prompted his oppofition were evident; Abeillard was young and youth, in fome circumftances, carries an impreffion with it, too powerful for the fchemes and wary circumfpection of age and experience.. After fix months of intrigue and conteft, the old profeffor gave way, and Abeillard entered Melun at the head of a numerous band of followers. The victory was fignal [*].

The fchools opened with eclat. The late oppofition had but given luftre to his name, and animation to his talents. His leffons were thronged: curiofity was on tiptoe to fee the youth, who had difcomfited the Goliath of Paris; and the moft brilliant fuccefs attended his exertions.

Thus having run, fome months, in the undifturbed enjoyment of public applaufe, when a mind lefs turbulent and ambitious would have repofed in the poffeffion of fame, Abeillard meditated new hoftilities againft his old mafter. Tranquillity was ill-adapted to his character; he breathed eafier in a ftorm; and the want of a rival was the want of a ftimulus, without which admiration itfelf had little power to pleafe.

[*] Hift. Calam.

The recollection of ill-ufage, the petulance of
youth, and, as he owns himfelf, an overweening
prefumption, aided, as may be imagined, by the
flattering inftigation of friends, urged him to this
extraordinary ftep. He left Melun, and advanced
to Corbeil, within five leagues of Paris [10].

De Champeaux heard of the approach of the
young adventurer with difmay and indignation:
it was bringing defiance even to his doors: and
what was a circumftance peculiarly irritating, this
beardlefs profeffor had arranged in fyftematic order
the various opinions of his mafter, and them he
attacked with all the acrimony of wit, and the
power of difputation. Nor fatisfied with frittering
into duft his ftrongeft arguments, on their ruins
he erected fyftems of his own, he formed new
plans of oppofition, and was throughout fupported
by the acclamations of his fcholars, who were
ready to go any lengths with a mafter, whom they
loved and admired.—De Champeaux was not idle:
if the enemy conquered, he was determined his
victory fhould be dearly bought. They met repeatedly at each other's fchool; and the road betwixt
Corbeil and Paris was crowded with their refpective fcholars, who, emulating the ardor of their
mafters, fought every occafion of fignalizing their
zeal and prowefs. Victory hung not long in fuf-

[10] Hift. Calam.

penfe; Abeillard made an eafy conqueft, and the enemy retired in confufion. The palm of victory waved proudly in his hand ". "

The reader will wifh to know what thofe important matters were, which could command fo much intereft, and in which the paffions of thoufands were engaged. A fuperficial view over the face of fociety, at all times, will tell him that, it matters not what the thing itfelf may be: but once raife the attention of men, and their paffions, as by a magic touch, will rufh forward into faction, whether it be to afcertain the juft dimenfions of a gewgaw, or to give away an empire.

The grand point then in debate, and which continued for centuries in high litigation, was, whether that which is *univerfal* in the mind has alfo a *real* exiftence in nature; that is, whether Peter and John, individuals of the human race, poffefs fo completely the totallity of rational nature, as to be only *accidentally* different men.—Champeaux maintained the affirmative, Abeillard the negative, queftion.—If the whole *effence* of humanity, objected the latter, be *fubftantially* in each individual, then are John and Peter the fame man; or, if all be in Peter, what is left for John? There is but one human fubftance, he urged, in nature, and of this all the individuals of the univerfe muft be

" Vie d'Abeil.

accounted

accounted modes.—He might likewife have infifted on the arguments, which have fince been enforced againft the doctrine of Spinofa; for the two opinions are very nearly allied.—If the fame human naturo be not *indivifibly* in Peter and John, replied Champeaux, they are not both men, for it is only the attribute of humanity which makes them what they are ".—He was not aware that thefe abftracted ideas had no exiftence out of his own mind; that they expreffed nothing which could be found in nature.—Had their notions been derived from this fource, the object of their refearches would have been fomething real, and mankind would not fo long have wandered in the regions of error or of romantic extravagance.

On the two notions, juft mentioned, were founded the refpective fyftems of the *nominalifts* and *realifts*, fects of fuch high renown in the chriftian fchools, that their difputes, for ages, feemed to have abforbed the ftrongeft exertions of human wit.—Many, and very fimilar, were the other queftions in agitation. Could their enume- ration poffibly give pleafure, it fhould not be with- held. Enough perhaps has been inftanced to damp the moft ardent curiofity: if not, I muft refer my reader to the fchoolmen, whofe volumes have come down to us, full and unadulterated as they fell from their pens.

" Vie d'Abeil. p. 25. Bayle, vol. i.

VOL. I. C

Abeillard now deemed himfelf the chofen minion
of fortune, and nothing, it feemed, could retard
his afcent to higher honors. But inceffant application had preyed on his health; his fibres were
yet too weak to fupport fo long a tenfion; and
delicacy of frame foon effected what the efforts of
de Champeaux had aimed at in vain. By the
advice of his phyficians, when all other means had
proved ineffectual, he left Corbeil, and retired to
his native country ".—It was well judged that
ceffation from labor, and the air of Britany, which
had given the firft tone to his conftitution, would
probably beft enfure his recovery.—Here he remained two long years, at a diftance, he obferves,
from all that was deareft to him, and only confoled
by the repeated affurances of his friends, that his
return was anxioufly wifhed for by all, whofe
fouls were enamoured of the love of wifdom.

During this period of retirement, every thing
was calm in the fchools of Paris. De Champeaux,
freed from the preffure of his rival, had leifure
to breathe in peace; and he looked forward towards church-preferment, as to the adequate
reward of his fervices. For fome time, he had been
archdeacon of Paris, a poft of dignity and truft.

At the times I am defcribing, the general face
of religion was much disfigured by private vices

" Hift. Calam.

and public crimes: nor did the conduct of its ministers merit less reprehension: on the contrary, the secular clergy, in particular, was ignorant and undisciplined, effeminate and licentious. To remedy the evil, as far as might be, recourse was often had to the cloisters: Here could be found men, endowed at least with more piety and learning, and these were promoted to the first ecclesiastical dignities. Hence the ambitious sometimes became monks; the humility of the profession, they knew, might lead to honors; and though the mitre should never press their brows, still, in the monastic life itself, there were posts of splendor and emolument, wherein vanity might be satisfied, and even ambition could find a pillow on which to repose.—With these views, it is said, de Champeaux entered the cloister. He chose for his retreat a small monastery, then out of the walls of Paris, and which, in process of time, became the celebrated convent of St. Victor. In the eye of the philosopher, to whom the definitions of universal nature were familiar, but little, it seems, was necessary to constitute a monk; for in his new habit he retained his old ways; the same lectures continued; he was contentious as before; and the little convent of St. Victor became a school of controversy and philosophic warfare [*],

[*] Hist. Calam.

BOOK
I.

To his logical difputations he, in a fhort time, fubjoined leffons on rhetoric, and thefe were followed by more important theological difcuffions. De Champeaux is faid to have been the firft mafter who had ventured to give public lectures in divinity, in the form of polemic difputations [11] : but when Abeillard was away, and his abilities, which, it muft be owned, were very great, had their full play, the whole range of fcience feemed placed within the eafy grafp of his comprehenfion.

He returns to
Paris.

Such were the events which had taken place at Paris, when Abeillard, in the vigor of revived health, returned from Britany. He was now twenty-eight years old. His mind alfo, genially refreflied by repofe and inward rumination on itfelf, had acquired a new fpring : he had extended, doubtlefs, his former train of ideas, had arranged them in frefh combinations, and had added confiderably to the old flock.—It is with the mind of man, as with the earth we tread on; her fruitful lap muft fometimes repofe from the harrow, or inflead of teeming with plenty, fhe will give us weeds, or her beft produce will be feeble and uninvigorating.—He came ftraight to Paris.

De Champeaux was in the quiet poffeffion of the lectures, juft mentioned, when Abeillard

[11] Vie d'Abeil.

re-appeared. It was a moment of some anxiety to
both; but the young man evidently showed an
indecision, which could not at once be unravelled. He weighed his situation; when, to the
surprise of every one, he again put himself under
the tuition of his old master, and frequented his
rhetorical lesson. There was a mystery in this
conduct: either he felt himself deficient in the
art, or he hoped to regain the favor of a person,
whose enmity, he had reason to suspect, might
prove an obstacle to his future progress, or it
was his wish perhaps to have it more easily in his
power to humble the man he hated. He himself
barely relates the fact.

De Champeaux, if he was ignorant of the human
heart, or if vanity had obscured his judgment,
might be flattered by this apparent submission.
The daring youth, who had braved him in the
schools and triumphed, now voluntarily courts
his instruction, and seems disposed to take wisdom
from his lips!—But the illusive dream soon vanished.
It could not be, that rivals, whose prejudices
were inveterate, whose opinions so widely varied,
and whose pursuits were the same, could meet
again, and really be friends. Abeillard once more
assailed his enemy in the open field of controversy,
(for though rhetoric was his leading object, he
frequented the other lessons,) and so irresistible
was the attack, particularly on the great point of

BOOK *universal essences*, which I have described, that de
I.   Champeaux, opiniutive and supported as he was,
       owned himself convinced, and publicly subscribed
       to the opinion of his adversary.—It might be the
       effect of conviction, of pusillanimity, or of a
       mind rendered lowly by the influence of the cowl.
       The public, at least, judged unfavorably of the
       step; his credit left him, his scholars withdrew,
       and it was even in agitation to forbid him the
       schools of philosophy [16].

       Abeillard knew how to conquer, and how to
       avail himself of victory: he received, with great
       marks of benevolence, the scholars of de Cham-
       peaux, and again opened his school with more
       splendor, and with more general approbation than
       ever. Very soon he was the sole professor in Paris,
       for he who had succeeded to de Champeaux,
       when he became a monk and retired to St. Victor,
       of his own accord waited on Abeillard, surrendered
       to him his chair of philosophy, and requested to
       be enrolled in the number of his disciples [17].—
       This may be regarded as the most brilliant epoch
       in the life of Abeillard. He rose every morning
       to the smiles of an approving public; and the
       church, at the same time, willing to testify the
       high opinion she entertained of his merit, pre-
       sented him with a canonicate in the cathedral of

       [16] Hist. Calam.   [17] Ibid.

Paris ".—It was a finecure, and the emoluments were beftowed on him without any further obligation ; for I do not find he was at all engaged in the ecclefiaftical ftate.

De Champeaux viewed with pain the bright funfhine, which feemed hourly to expand round his adverfary : he was determined to obftruct its fpread; but as he was cautious to attack a reputation which, he knew, he could not fully, he hit on an expedient which fucceeded.—Though the perfon, I have mentioned, had refigned the honors of his chair to Abeillard, he had ftill retained the falary, and was therefore in fact the regular profeffor. This man he accufed of crimes and mifdemeanors, and fo far made good his charges, that he was removed from his office, and another was chofen in his place, who, it may well be imagined, bore little kindnefs towards Abeillard, or wifhed to patronife his renown ".

Abeillard was unprepared for this wily ftratagem, and once more he found himfelf neceffitated to retire to Melun. To be outwitted by an enemy he defpifed was a mortifying circumftance; in other regards, the event only ferved to enhance his fame. The moft prejudiced began to fufpect what the motives were which had inftigated the conduct of de Champeaux, even from

" Vie d'Abeil. p. 28.   " Hift. Calam.

C 4

BOOK the firſt commencement of hoſtilities; the number
I. of his friends increaſed; his lectures were received
with a more marked applauſe, if poſſible; and
in triumph of foul he applied to himſelf the
line of Ovid,

Summa petit livor, perflant altiſſima venti.

De Rem. Am. l. 1.

Even the beſt friends of de Champeaux were
ſevere in their reflections. Monk as he now is,
ſaid they, he ſhould retire from the world; the
noiſe of the ſchools and the diſſipating ſcenes of
Paris, accord ill with his new profeſſion; woods
and ſolitude would give an edge to his devotion,
and diſpoſe him for a nearer intercourſe with
heaven [*].—Stung by theſe reproaches, he ſaw it
was time to give way, and having prevailed on
the monks to accompany him, they all removed
from St. Victor to a country-retirement more remote from the city.

Abeillard, hearing of the enemy's flight, apprehended he might return without further moleſta-
tion, and again he turned his face towards the
capital. But as the ſchools, within the walls,
were poſſeſſed by the new profeſſor, he advanced
only as far as the mount of St. Genevieve, there
halted, and encompaſſed by his followers, with

[*] Hiſt. Calam.

all expedition , made the neceſſary preparations
for a vigorous aſſault on the enemy. —The mount
of St. Genevieve has long been rendered famous
by a large abbey, which covers its ſummit ; nor
is it leſs famous on account of the ſuperſtitious
veneration which , even at this day, the inhabitants
of the moſt diſſipated, the moſt enlightened, and
perhaps moſt unbelieving city in the univerſe,
practiſe round the ſhrine of the holy ſhepherdeſs,
who has given her name to the mountain.—When
I ſpeak of ſuperſtitious veneration , it is clear I
mean ſuch abuſes, as every traveller has witneſſed,
and every good man has lamented.

In the retirement of his country-cell, de Champeaux being informed of the ſtep his rival had
taken, inſtantly took the alarm, and with his
whole community returned in haſte to St. Victor,
reſolved, ſays Abeillard, either to raiſe the ſiege,
or to ſupport, at all perils , the fortune of his
friend. His preſence , however , produced not
the intended effect. For no ſooner was the voice
of de Champeaux again heard in the ſchools,
than the new profeſſor, whoſe talents, it appears,
were very ſlender, found himſelf deſerted by his
ſcholars, and the two rival philoſophers remained
the ſole champions on the field ''.

I leave it to the reader , whoſe mind perhaps

'' Hiſt. Calam.

BOOK
I.

may have been warmed by the novelty of an uncommon ſtory, to picture to himſelf thoſe ſcenes
of acrimony, and pertinacious diſputation, which
rapidly ſucceeded to one another among the ſcholars of theſe able maſters and the two heroes themſelves. Abeillard is rather modeſt in his narration:
but, ſays he, I think, I may boldly take to myſelf
the words of Ajax,

> Si quæritis hujus
> Fortunam pugnæ, non ſum ſuperatus ab illo.
> Ovid. Met. l. xiii.

He goes again
into Britany.

In the midſt of this high tide of deſperate con-
troverſy, he received a letter from his mother,
requeſting he would, without delay, come into
Britany, on ſome family-buſineſs, which concerned
her much. He obeyed the ſummons with an alacrity that did him credit. It was leaving the poſt
of honor at a criſis, when the general aſpect of
the day ſeemed to promiſe a certainty of ſucceſs:
but the call of nature came nearer to his heart than
all the honors, however great his ambition might
be, which fortune ſeemed prepared to ſhower upon
him. When the heart of a wiſe man ceaſes to
vibrate to the gentle impreſſions of humanity, he
becomes a monſter, and ſhould retire to the
woods. — The mother of Abeillard, after the
retreat of her huſband from the world, now meditated the ſame ſtep: it was the faſhion of the times:

and the previous fettlement of fome wordly matters feems to have been the bufinefs which called Abeillard from the fchools. Whatever it was, his ftay in Britany was fhort; he returned, but he found, to his furprife, that de Champeaux, during the interval of his abfence, had been decorated with the mitre of Chalons [11].

Here I fhall leave this extraordinary man. He has exhibited a fcene not incurious in itfelf; not from the difplay of an uncommon character, for his paffions were the common paffions of man; nor becaufe, faint-like as he is faid to have been, he purfued the darling object of his ambition with unceafing ardor, for this is no unufual thing, at all times; but merely becaufe the bufinefs, in which he was engaged, differs from the purfuits of modern habits, and is therefore novel to us. Every man, whofe heart is not at eafe, looks round for what he wants, and if his character be peculiar, he will feize on a peculiar object. But, in many regards, it would furely have been well for the common interefts of humanity, had all the ardent fpirit of the eleventh century been as innocently employed, as was that of de Champeaux. Europe was in a ftate of fermentation.

Abeillard, returned to the fchools, faw nothing any longer worth contending for: He ftood with-

He refolves to ftudy divinity.

[11] Hift. Calam. Fleury, &c.

out a rival; but then he stood without feeling
that thrill of pleasure, which success gives to animated exertions: besides, this rival, who had
given way before him and owned his inferiority,
had first reached, notwithstanding, the goal of
his wishes: to the honors he had obtained, he
thought perhaps that he himself had equal, if not
better pretensions. — Disappointment would be
the consequence of these reflections; and when
this happens, a disgust of former pursuits often
follows, whilst the heart sinks from its expansion,
and hardly seems to fill the breast. — Moreover,
philosophy had no longer any novelty in his eyes:
he had seen her, and that familiarly, in all the
forms, whether of art or nature, which she could
then exhibit. Reflection might also have told
him, that there were other studies more deserv-
ing of attention, wherein an object could be
found more adequate to his talents; and in these
thoughts the advice of a parent might have confirmed him, whom he greatly honored, and who
then was turning her back on the empty employments of a vain world. — Abeillard assented
to these suggestions of reason, and at once resolved to apply himself to the study of theology ".

The reader has gone with me over more than
the twenty last years of the eleventh century,
and I have confined his view barely to those

" Hist. Calam.

tranfactions, in which Abeillard, the hero of thefe pages, bore a principal part. The introduction of large objects into the fmall fcene, I was de-lineating, would have had a prepofterous effect; it would have deftroyed that harmony or unity of defign, which pleafes beft. But, during this fhort period, very great events had agitated the chriftian world: them I will now bring forward; they will give an agreeable relief to the eye; and we will review them, on a large fcale, with the unprejudiced coolnefs of hiftorical candor.

Hildebrand, the famous Gregory the feventh, then wore the triple crown. He had been edu-cated at Cluni, a French monaftery of high renown, in the feverity of monaftic difcipline; had then rifen to the firft dignities in the church; and dur-ing the pontificates of five fucceffive Popes, had been honored with their confidence in the dif-charge of the moft arduous bufinefs. — It is well known what a torrent of vice had then fpread it-felf over the face of chriftendom: to ftem this, in vain had every effort been made, which honeft virtue and chriftian zeal could fuggeft. Hildebrand, with the keen fenfibility of a virtuous mind, had long viewed the fallen ftate of religion, and he afcended the Papal throne, with the unanimous approbation of all orders of the Roman church, big with vaft defigns of reformation. " We chufe " Hildebrand for the true vicar of Chrift, " (they

BOOK are the words ufed at this election,) "a man of
I.   " much learning, of great piety, of prudence,
        " juftice, fortitude, and religion. He is modeft,
        " abftemious, and chafte; regular in the difcipline
        " of his family, hofpitable to the poor, and from
        " his tender years nurfed in the bofom of our holy
        " church: to him we give thofe powers of fupre-
        " macy, which Peter once received from the mouth
        " of God ". "

The fource of the evils, he lamented, lay, it
was evident, in the general corruption of manners,
in the unbounded fway of paffion, and in the abufe
of power? With an intrepidity of foul, that perhaps was never equalled, he dared fingly to oppofe
this multitudinous enemy, and he called the fovereigns of Europe to his tribunal. The motives
which led him on, and the habits of ftern virtue,
which had fteeled his character, excluded almoft
the poffibility of fufpicion, that he himfelf perhaps
was arrogating a power, which belonged not to
him, and from the abufe of which even greater
evils might enfue, than thofe he aimed to fupprefs.
Minds of the wideft comprehenfion may be fometimes fo engroffed by a fingle object, as to be infenfible to the moft obvious deductions, which
reafon in vain holds up before them. But the
mif-conceptions of Gregory were thofe of a great

" Platina and others.

man, and his errors were, in part, the errors of the age.

To effectuate more completely the fchemes he had in view, he conceived the bold defign of making himfelf fole monarch of the earth. The concerns of Europe, whether ecclefiaftical or civil, would then be brought within his own cognizance; he fhould diftribute favors, as merit might feem to call for them; and he would difpofe of crowns; which, too often, he obferved, fell upon the heads of the unworthy, or of men who knew not the proper ufe of power.

Enthroned in the chair of the humble fifherman, Gregory put his hand to the work. The fimoniacal difpofal of church-livings was a crying fin, which called aloud for redrefs, and he hefitated not to aim the firft blow at the very root of the diforder, though it lay in the rapacious breaft of power; and in the courts of Princes.—The incontinence of the clergy was another foul ftain on religion: for the fons of God feeing the daughters of men that they were fair, took to them helpmates from among all that they chofe. The ftern pontiff had no indulgence for this weaknefs of his brethren.

During the twelve years of his reign he held eleven councils at Rome, the object of all which was, the fuppreffion of the crimes, I have mentioned, or to enforce the execution of decrees or

difcipline, or to confirm, by a more folemn
fanction, the fentences of excommunication and
depofition which, in the plenitude of his fuppofed
power, he had pronounced againft the obftinate
and refractory.

In two fynods he compelled Berengarius, who
had innovated in the doctrine of the Lord's Supper,
to abjure his opinions, and to fubfcribe to the
ancient faith.—The general oppofition, which the
dogmatical fentiments of this man excited, proves
at leaft their novelty in the eleventh century,

Studious of reconciling the long divided churches
of the Eaft and Weft, he had purpofed to proceed
himfelf to Conftantinople, and to bring the grand
controverfy to iffue. The difturbances of Europe
forbad it.—He wrote to the Grecian Emperor, who
had implored his fuccour that, at the head of
the powers of the Weft, he would march to
his affiftance ; and he conjured the German
Henry and William Duke of Burgundy to join
him in the enterprife ".—The idea did honor to
the magnanimous fpirit of Gregory ; but twenty
more years were to elapfe before Europe would
be prepared to fend her holy warriors againft the
Infidel powers of the Eaftern world.

He reprimanded Salomon King of Hungary,
that he had dared to accept the inveftiture of his

" Nat. Alex. fæc. xi.

realm

realm from the hand of the Emperor, and not
from Rome. Hungary, faid he, was rendered feudatory of the holy fee by Stephen, the beſt of her kings, and your right of holding the fceptre is from hence [14].

He wrote to the kings of Denmark, of Sweden, and of Norway, reproving what had been ill done, and urging them to the due difcharge of their duties in the fupport of religion, and in procuring the welfare of their people; but particularly he preffes on their attention a filial obedience to the apof-tolic fee [15].

The murder of Staniſlaus, biſhop of Cracow, he revenged on the Poliſh king and the other perpetrators of the crime, in the moſt fignal manner. In execration of the deed, the whole kingdom was laid under an interdict, the king de-prived of all regal power, and his fubjects abfolved from their allegiance. None of the fons of thofe, who either aided or advifed the crime, faid he, ſhall be promoted to holy orders to the end of the fourth generation [16].

The kingdom of Spain, he pretended, had, from time immemorial, belonged to the Roman church; and when the count de Ronci applied to him for permiffion to retain the lands he might conquer from the Saracens, who then poffeffed them; he granted his prayer, on condition, he ſhould hold

[14] Fleury, vol. xiii. [15] Nat. Alex. fæc. xi. [16] Ibid.

BOOK
I.

them in the name of St. Peter. But I would rather, he obferved, they fhould remain in the hands of the infidels, than that chriftians fhould poffefs them, who might refufe to do homage to the holy fee ".

Alfonfus, king of Caftile, who had married the near relation of his firft wife, he threatened with excommunication, if he dared to cohabit any longer with her; and he admonifhed him to remove the evil counfellors, who had advifed him perverfely.   " Weighing, with awful " refolution, fays he, the value of earthly " poffeffions, it is then, I think, that a bifhop " beft merits his name, when in the caufe of " juftice, he fuffers perfecution. In obedience " to the laws of heaven, I will rather be hated " by the wicked, than flatter their defires, and " incur the anger of an irritated God ". "

To Dalmatia, to the ftates of Venice, and to Sardinia, he wrote in the fame ftyle of a judge and their fupreme governor. — Even to the inhofpitable clime of Ruffia he extended his monarchical jurifdiction.   " Your fon, fays he " to king Demetrius, has been with me, " requefting that I would make over your " kingdom to him, in the name of St. Peter. " His petition appeared juft, and I granted it ". "

The fons of count Raymond had quarrelled:

" Fleury, vol. xiii. " Nat. Alex. fæc. xi. " Fleury, ibid.

Gregory, as the umpire between contending
princes, undertook to reconcile them. " Tell
" them, fays he, that, if they difobey my orders,
" and continue enemies, I will deprive them of
" the protection of St. Peter: them and their
" abettors I will retrench from the fociety of
" chriftians: from that moment, their arms fhall
" be fuccefslefs in war, nor fhall they ever
" profper "."

William, our Norman conqueror, he treated
with unufual lenity; he fpeaks of his virtues, of
his moderation, and his juftice; and becaufe he
had fhown more refpect, than other princes,
towards the holy fee, his regal power, he thinks
fhould be more mildly handled. But when he
fent his legate into England to demand an oath
of fealty to himfelf and fucceffors, and to urge the
more regular payment of the fubfidy due to Rome,
the monarch anfwered, that the money fhould be
remitted; " but as to the oath, faid he, I
" neither have nor will make it, becaufe I have
" never promifed it, nor do I find that it was
" ever made by my predeceffors to yours. " —
The pontiff was irritated; " it is his fubmiffion,
" and not his money, that I value, faid he; "
but he acquiefced: he feemed to be awed by
William, and probably admired in him that
boldnefs of fpirit, which, from the dukedom of

" Fleury, vol. xiii.

D 2

Normandy, had raifed him to the throne of
England ".

The fame was not his moderation towards
Philip, king of France. Hearing that he had
refufed to admit to their fees fome bifhops, who
had been canonically chofen, he addreffed a letter
to the French prelates, expreffive of his ftrongeft
indignation: " either your king, faid he, fhall
" ceafe from his fimoniacal conduct, or the realm
" of France, ftruck by a general anathema, fhall
" withdraw from his obedience, unlefs they
" rather chufe to renounce their chriftianity. "
Philip gave way. — Afterwards, in a letter to the
monarch himfelf, he fays : " reflect, Sir, how
" great was the glory of your anceftors, as long as
" they continued faithful to the church, and
" protected its rights: but no fooner, in a change
" of manners, have the divine and human laws
" been trampled on, than your power and
" celebrity are no more. The important duties
" of my charge will often compel me to repeat
" thefe truths to you, and fometimes perhaps in
" feverer language. " — Philip had feized by
violence the property of fome Italian merchants :
Gregory commanded him to reftore it; fhould he
neglect to do it, he wrote to the count of
Poitiers, that it was his intention to remove him
from his throne. " Should he perfevere in his

" Fleury, vol. xiii.

" iniquities, we will fever him and all thofe who
" fhall obey him as their king , from the
" communion of the faithful ; and every day
" fhall this anathema be renewed on the altar of
" St. Peter. We have borne his crimes too long;
" but now were his power equal to that which
" the emperors of Rome practifed on the martyrs,
" no human fear fhould with-hold our vengeance
" any longer ''."

But it was with Henry the Fourth, emperor
of Germany, that was the grand quarrel, and
here we fhall fee marked, in the ftrongeft colors
the magnanimous and proud fpirit of Gregory.
What firft raifed the indignation of the zealous
pontiff, was the fimoniacal diftribution of bene-
fices, publicly practifed by Henry; and he was
accufed of various other crimes. The pope exerted
all his powers to ftem the raging torrent; he
advifed , he expoftulated, he reprimanded, and
he threatened. It was in vain; confpiracies were
formed againft him, his perfon was feized, but he was
refcued by the timely interference of the Roman
populace. Under pain of anathema, he then
ordered Henry to appear before him at Rome,
and he fixed the day for his appearance. The
emperor difobeyed the fummons, convoked an
affembly at Worms ; Gregory is accufed of
crimes, as unfounded, as they are fcandalous

** Fleury, vol. xiii.

BOOK
I.

and the fentence of depofition is pronounced againſt him. On the other hand, the pope calls a fynod at Rome, where the prince is folemnly excommunicated and depofed, and his ſubjects are forbidden to obey him. The fentence was in thefe words.— "Peter, prince of the apoſtles,
" liſten to thy fervant, whom thou haſt tutored
" from his youth, and whom, to the prefent
" hour, thou haſt freed from the hands of the
" wicked, who hate me, becaufe I am faithful
" to thee. Thou canſt witnefs, and with thee
" can witnefs the holy mother of Chriſt, and
" thy brother Paul, that unwillingly I was
" compelled to mount this holy throne. Rather
" would I have worn out my life in exile, than
" have ufurped thy feat to gain glory and the
" praife of mortals. By thy favor has the care
" of the chriſtian world been committed to me;
" from thee I have the power of binding and
" of loofening. Refting on this affurance, for
" the honor and fupport of the church, in
" the name of God the Father almighty, of his
" Son, and of the Holy Ghoſt, I depofe Henry,
" who raſhly and infolently has raifed his arm
" againſt thy church, from all imperial and
" regal power, and his fubjects I abfolve from all
" allegiance to him. For it is meet that he, who
" aims to retrench the majeſty of thy church,
" ſhould be defpoiled of his own honors ". "

" Plat. Fleury, &c.

It was the firſt time that ſuch a ſentence had
been pronounced againſt a ſovereign prince. —
Moderate men were ſhocked at the procedure,
and talked of terms of accommodation. " I am
" no enemy to concord, replied Gregory, let
" Henry firſt make his peace with heaven :
" nor did I proceed to this rigor, till all other
" means had been tried in vain."— Some obſerved
that a prince ſhould not be excommunicated.—
" And when Chriſt committed his church to
" Peter, anſwered the pontiff ſternly, ſaying,
" feed my ſheep, did he except kings? "

The nobles of Germany, whom the crimes and
miſconduct of Henry had exaſperated, reſolve not
to loſe ſo favorable an occaſion of reſenting
their injuries, and publicly announce their
intention of electing another maſter. To ward off
the blow, Henry croſſed the Alps, hoping by
this apparent ſubmiſſion, to appeaſe alſo the
anger of Gregory. Arrived at Canuſium, a caſtle
belonging to the counteſs Matilda, where the
pope then was, he diſmiſſed his guard, laid down
every enſign of royalty, and barefooted, in the
humble garb of a penitent, he preſented himſelf
at the gates. He was refuſed admittance. It was
winter, and the ſeaſon was ſevere. Here he
remained, ſilent and ſubmiſſive, till the riſing of
the fourth ſun, when, at the entreaty of Matilda
and others, he was admitted to the preſence of

D 4

BOOK I. Gregory. An accommodation took place, and his abfolution was pronounced, on condition, that he fhould ever remain obedient to the holy fee, that he fhould appear before his accufers to anfwer to their charges, and that he fhould abide by the final award of Rome. Henry affented [44].

In the prefence of the people, Gregory then celebrated the facred myfteries; and after the confecration, whilft the emperor and his affiftants flood round the altar; " I have been accufed, " faid he, (turning towards them with the holy " bread in his hand,) by you and your party, " of various crimes, as well before as fince my " promotion to the chair of St. Peter. They " that know me can fufficiently atteft my innocence; " but that the world may know it; let this body " of our Lord, which you fee, be a witnefs to " me: if I am guilty, may I die!" Uttering thefe words, he put a part of the facred bread into his mouth, and fwallowed it.—The folemn and unexpected action ftruck the affembly, and their acclamations founded through the caftle. The pontiff then addreffed the aftonifhed prince. " My fon, the remaining portion is for you. The " German nobles have accufed you, and they " demand that you be judged; but how uncertain " are the judgments of men! If you feel yourfelf " innocent, at once fave your own honor,

[44] Fleury, ibid.

" filence your enemies, and make me your friend.
God fhall be your judge." So faying, he advanced
towards him : the emperor fhrunk back, and with-
drawing, for a moment, with his friends, it
was determined that he fhould not expofe himfelf
to the tremendous ordeal ".

The Lombards, looking with indignation on
this bafe fubmiffion of their king, refolve to give
their allegiance to his fon, who was yet an infant.
Henry takes the alarm, and breaks through. the
treaty he had juft contracted. — But the German
ftates affemble at Forcheim, and being informed
by the pope's legates, that the fentence of
depofition againft Henry had not been revoked,
though he had been taken into communion, they
elect for their king Rodolphus duke of Suabia. —
Gregory, to whom fufficient attention had not
been paid in this important ftep, for fome time
feemed to remain neuter between the contending
factions. He received their ambaffadors, who
came to petition that the artillery of the vatican
might play on their refpective enemies. The
pontiff only anfwered, that they fhould firft lay
down their arms, and he would judge their caufes.
But inaction ill-accorded with his reftlefs difpofition:
he convoked another fynod, wherein Henry was
again excommunicated and depofed, and his
dominions folemnly transferred to Rodolphus. To

" Fleury, ibid.

the new king he promifed victory; and feemed to
predict death and fuccefslefs arms to the depofed
monarch. Heaven was inattentive to his voice; for
after repeated. battles, Rodolphus himfelf fell.
Henry then marched to Rome, accompanied by
Guibertus, archbifhop of Ravenna, whom he had
chofen anti-pope, and laid fiege to the caftle of
St. Angelo. The tiara trembled on the head of
Gregory; and he was on the point of falling into
the hands of his enemy, when the renowned
Robert Guifcard, who was become the laft friend
of the pontiff, marched from the Eaft to his
deliverance. The fiege was raifed, and Henry,
whom his anti-pope had juft crowned emperor,
retired. But the Romans, worn down by troubles
and the devaftations of war, began to treat
Gregory as the author of their misfortunes. His
high fpirit could ill-brook this reverfe of fortune:
he withdrew to Salerno, where he died the year
following, in 1085 [*].

Nor was he more indulgent to the vices of
churchmen, than to the excefles of princes. Bifhops
and archbifhops, whofe fins were flagrant, he
excommunicated and depofed in all quarters of
the globe, and his cenfures fell, like the hail in
March, wherever vice dared to rear its head. But
to the virtuous he was indulgent, and he rewarded
their merit.

[*] Platina, Fleury, &c.

Notwithftanding this extraordinary feverity of
character and conduct, Gregory found friends in
the fofter fex. Agnes, mother to Henry, and
Matilda his relation, countefs of Tufcany, admired
him as the greateft and beft of men: nor was
theirs a fterile admiration. The countefs made
over to the holy fee all her poffeffions; which
were confiderable, in Lombardy and Tufcany;
her purfe and intereft were ever devoted to
Gregory; and her armies were ready to march at
his call. As might be expected, his enemies, who
were numerous, and particularly the churchmen,
whofe incontinence he chaftifed with a fevere
hand, were loud in their reflections; but fo
irreproachable and fo exemplary was the tenor
of his life, that malevolence itfelf could not
tarnifh its luftre ".

Such was Gregory the Seventh. It has been his
lot, as it has been that of all great men, to be
admired by fome, and to be cenfured by others.
Thefe reflect not that he lived in the eleventh
century, when the manners of the age, and the
ideas of men, were fo different from thofe of the
prefent day. We generally meafure the conduct
of others at a very unfair ftandard. — The notions
of Gregory were fome of them, I confefs, even
then novel; but they were principally grounded

" Platina, Fleury, &c.

on a newly-difcovered collection of decrees, to which the weak criticifm of the times gave great authenticity. The high powers he exercifed were not difputed in their principle; he was even urged to the ufe of them, as contending factions judged they might be ferviceable to their views.

If we contemplate Gregory with the fame eyes, with which we look on an Alexander or on a Cæfar, I think, we may be difpofed to raife him far above the level of thofe mighty conquerors. With them he aimed at univerfal empire, but with views far more meritorious than theirs. His great ambition was to extirpate vice from the earth, and oger its furface to extend the benign influence of that religion which himfelf practifed and revered. Before a mind, fwelling with this noble project, was it not natural, that princes and fceptred kings fhould fink into infignificancy? He would treat them as impediments, which lay in the way of his defigns. Gregory, at the head of armies, would have called after him the admiration of pofterity : we view him in another light, becaufe habituated to appreciate what are called great qualities, by the conqueft of kingdoms and the overthrow of armies, we have not eyes for other talents, or for achievements formed in another order of things.

But though this power of Gregory, which his successors, as circumstances favored, long strove to support, could sometimes check the progress of vice, yet could it not, by any means, complete the object they had in view. The evil was too inveterate. — Europe was divided into an infinity of petty states, the heads over which lived in perpetual hostilities. Thus was formed a scale of oppression: the strongest became the tyrant; but the weakest also had vassals, on whom the hand of despotism pressed with all the weight it had: — General dissipation, and the consequence of it general indolence, gave birth to the basest species of crimes; and had not the call of arms roused them into action, the state of humanity would have been greatly more deplorable than it was. The disorders of a relaxed habit are often the most fatal.

When we listen to the descriptions, exaggerated it may be presumed, which some historians give of the kingdom of France, the mind draws back with horror. Yet in the midst of this scene, the light and airy Philip indulged himself in all the joys of wine and women. Tired of his queen, he forcibly took to his arms Bertrada, the wife of the count of Anjou, and he called upon the laws to give their sanction to the iniquitous deed.

BOOK
I. The thunders of the vatican rolled over his head and fell; but he had addrefs enough to ward off the worft effect of excommunication, which was depofition, and the confequent defection of his fubjects. — The rapacity of the great barons was infatiable; and the bifhop¹, thofe meek-eyed minifters of peace, bound on the helmet, and with the arm of flefh defended the rights of the church and their own poffeffions ¹¹.

State of
England. In England the general afpect of affairs was more pleafing, than in other parts of Europe. The conqueft, though humbling to the Britifh fpirit, was productive of happy effects. It ferved to roufe the fallen character of the nation : there was fomething in the Norman blood well adapted to coalefce with the Englifh conftitution, and to improve it; a new tide of life began to flow in our veins. Till then, almoft unknown and little important in the connexion of Europe, England, like a new conftellation, appeared above the horizon, and foon rofe to the firft magnitude by its learning, by its commerce, by its conquefts. — William, indeed, was a tyrant; but what conqueror was ever otherwife? The feverity of his reign was the natural effect of circumftances: he had to break the proud fpirit of his new fubjects,

¹¹ Daniel, Fleury, &c.

which, left to itself, muſt ever have fermented into plots and inſurrections ; he had to ſhow them that it was not the capricious will of fortune which had put the ſceptre into his hand , but that he owed it to the ſure aſcendency of his own abilities and arm, and therefore that he was able to maintain it; and he had to reward thoſe brave companions, who had bled and conquered by his ſide. In his friends he ſaw merit, which, he could not deſcry in his enemies, and what wonder , if the poſſeſſions of the latter were ſeized to enrich them ; but even here he wiſhed to ſupport the outward forms of juſtice ".

His ſon and ſucceſſor, William Rufus, was a tyrant by principle, and never perhaps did a more ſtern and undiſciplined heart beat in the human breaſt.

Lanfranc and Anſelm , at this period ſucceſſively filled the ſee of Canterbury; men of ſuperior talents, of ſuperior piety, and of ſuperior fortitude. By them religion was ſupported , whilſt its mild influence began to ſoften the ferocious manners of the age ; and learning, under their protection, again dared to rear its head. England looked up to theſe venerable prelates, and in the milder light which beamed from their virtues ſeemed to diſcover ſomething that might be admired,

" Hume and others.

BOOK and fomething that might be imitated. All was
I.   not abforbed in the blaze of martial fplendor.

Unfortunately, the notions of prerogative and
exclufive privileges, which, originating from the
chair of St. Peter, foon took poffeffion of the
breafts of churchmen, precipitated thefe worthy
men into difputes with their fovereigns, from
which fatal evils enfued. Thus was obftructed
the fpread of thofe many advantages which, in
other circumftances, England would have derived
from their talents and their virtues. When I read
the invectives of modern hiftorians againft fuch
men; I own, I blufh : for their lives were
without reproach, and the motives of their
conduct, grounded on the approved maxims of
the age, were dictated to them by honor and
fincerity. Had they lived at fome earlier or fome
later period, differently would they have acted;
but in the eleventh century, not to have
conformed to its principles, would have been a
bafe furrender of rights and privileges, which
every idea of their minds then told them to
revere ".

Though the hiftorian, whofe bufinefs it fhould be
to detail the events of this period, and to portray
the different characters, whom he fhould find
deferving of great praife or of great reprehenfion,

" Fleury, Nat. Alex. fæc. xi. quoting original authors.

might

might find ample matter for his pen, and in that
matter, ample amufement for his readers; yet is
there one grand event which feems to occupy
fo large a fpace in the eye of the beholder, that
all other objects dwindle away before it.—I have
laid what may he deemed fufficient to exhibit the
general features of the times; that folely is my
object; the remaining delineation will develope
what elfe may be thought requifite to complete
the portrait.

Alter Conftantine, in the fourth century, had
given celebrity to the chriftian religion, and by
his care, and that of his mother Helen, Paleftine
in particular, the native land of our Saviour,
had been decorated with many monuments of
their piety, and the holy places at Jerufalem had
been brought out to more public infpection; a
certain inftinctive veneration for that diftant and
venerable fpot feized on the minds of men. The
foil, on which Jefus Chrift had flood, they
deemed bleffed; and what feems more extraordinary, fays a writer who does not always reafon
juftly, even the inftruments which had been
ufed in the fhedding of his blood. What man,
continues he, left to the free impulfe of humanity, would imprint his kiffes on the axe, that
had let out the life of his deareft friend ? The
new impreffion was however made, and in many

it was founded on ideas of the sincerest piety. It
may be called *new*, because it seems to have had
no place in the minds of those christians, who
were contemporary to the period when the great
tragedy was performed.

Constantine, as his historians relate, had seen
a miraculous apparition of the cross; and under
that sign he had conquered. From that time, the
cross was no longer a mark of infamy; it waved
on the banners of his army; and the Roman eagle
was taught to stoop before it. Out of compliment to the master of the world, had no pious
impulse helped the bias, it was natural that respect
should be shown to this favored sign.

Pilgrimages to the holy land soon became
frequent, and soon they were fashionable. Even
after the destruction of the Western empire, the
journey was attended with no peculiar difficulties,
because the new kingdoms which arose continued
to profess the christian faith. But in the seventh
century the great change took place; when the
disciples of Mahomet, a people divided from us
by religion, by language, and by manners, rose,
like a dark cloud, in the East, and spread
themselves over the surface of many kingdoms. Still
were the pilgrims permitted to resort to Jerusalem:
the pious travellers came not empty-handed; it was
besides a species of devotion, of which the infidels

were themſelves rather fond; and curioſity would be pleaſed at the ſight of ſuch a motly concourſe of ſtrangers from every corner of Europe. Mecca, on its brighteſt days, could hardly boaſt of a fairer ſpectacle.

Thus, for many years, continued this wondrous practice; when the Saracens maſters of the land, no longer pleaſed with the idle ſcene, or irritated by the miſconduct of the pilgrims, or apprehenſive, not without reaſon, that enthuſiaſm might at laſt prompt them to meditate deſigns againſt the ſtate ; began to ſhow them fewer marks of kindneſs, and even oppreſſed thoſe of the chriſtian name, who were ſettled amongſt them. Of this oppreſſion and of their own ill-treatment, they told a piteous and exaggerated tale, on their return to Europe; and dreadful indeed they ſaid, it was, that the holy places ſhould be poſſeſſed by the declared foes to the religion of Chriſt ! To attempt their reſcue however was an act of ſolemn chivalry, which only the lapſe of ages could bring to maturity.

The Grecian emperors, indeed, were ever at war with the Ottoman powers; but it was to defend their own frontiers, which the enemy daily invaded with ſucceſs. The blood ran back upon the heart, and the proud towers of Conſtantinople

trembled for their own fecurity. It was no time
to think of foreign conquefts. — The Goths,
the Lombards, the Francs, and other nations,
which now rofe into power, in the Weft, were
embroiled in domeftic quarrels, or occupied with
fchemes of felf-prefervation. Even from the
infidels themfelves they had reafon to fear the
moft ruinous incurfions : already they were in
poffeffion of the moft fertile provinces of Spain,
and the fate of Spain feemed to hover over the
other ftates of Europe. Common policy fhould
have told them, that the beft fecurity againft
the inroads of an enemy is, to carry war into
his own territories. But, I have faid, that the
European powers were themfelves unfettled.

It was only towards the clofe of the eleventh
century, that the Weftern chriftians conceived
the defign of a general confederation againft the
infidels of the Eaft. Gregory the feventh, the man
whofe virtues I praifed, whofe abilities I admired,
but whofe extravagancies I cenfured, feems firft
to have adopted the grand idea. Hiftorians tell
us [11], that he was moved to it by the melancholy
recital of the fufferings of the Chriftians, who
groaned under the Ottoman yoke. It might indeed
be that, knowing how powerfully a tale of diftrefs
operated on the human mind, he would not lofe

[11] Fleury and others.

its effect; and therefore urged it as an efficacious motive , whereby to accomplish more eafily his defigns. But he was too wife a man, I think, to give much weight, in his own mind, to a circum-ftance in itfelf fo trifling. Thefe chriftians were not numerous, and might readily have withdrawn from the hand which oppreffed them. Nor can I for a moment fuppofe, he would deign to give a fingle thought to the fuggeftion, that, by marching into the Eaft , he fhould be able to give protection to the pilgrims, or facilitate their wild emigrations into Paleftine. Gregory had other views. The infidel powers were become terrible to Europe; their depredations were feared upon every maritime coaft; they had landed in Italy, and infulted the gates of Rome.

Europe, I have alfo faid, was cruelly lacerated by internal wars ; the hand of every man was armed againft his brother; nor did it feem, in the ordinary courfe of things, that this deplorable fcene could be brought to a conclufion. They had had recourfe indeed to a fingular expedient, which was called the *Truce of God*, whereby it was forbidden, under pain of excommunication, to make any attack on a private enemy, from the fetting of the fun on Wednefday to its rifing on Monday morning. This was fome relief—

E 3

BOOK I. Commerce and agriculture, the finews and the wealth of ftates, were little known ; or thofe thoufand arts of peace, which give employment to the more populous nations of modern times. — But could the arms, which chriftians ufed for mutual deftruction, be turned againft a common enemy, the evils of domeftic difcord would ceafe, and Europe might again profper and be happy ".

When in this light we view the crufades, they will not perhaps appear to have been dictated by that wild enthufiafm, to which generally they are afcribed. Not that I mean to infinuate that the multitude or their leaders were influenced by fuch rational motives : thefe can only belong to fuch men as Gregory or to Urban his fucceffor. The marching crufaders waved their banners under a more animating impulfe. They viewed themfelves as the chofen foldiers of the Lord : they looked to the land of Paleftine, as to a country they had a right to occupy, not reflecting, if the prefent poffeffors were ejected, that it fhould devolve to the Jews as an old inheritance ; and they were promifed that, in the blood of the unbelieving muffulmen, their own crimes fhould be cancelled.

" Fleury, difc. 6.

To the expedition, of which I shall now speak, had been a curious prelude in 1064, when seven thousand Germans, at the head of whom was Sigefroi, archbishop of Mayence, in a body took up the pilgrim's staff, and marched towards Jerusalem. They were attacked, even on good Friday, by a superior band of twelve thousand Arabs, and, after a stout defence, were on the point of falling a prey to the rapacious infidels, when unexpectedly, at the rising of the sun on Easter Sunday, they were rescued by an army of Turks, and conducted, under a strong escort, to the walls of Jerusalem [11]!

When the minds of men, from a concurrence of circumstances, have been long exposed to certain impressions — it matters not with what disgust or even horror they were at first received — gradually they become familiarized with them, and reason, or what by them is called reason, will soon be disposed to give them its solemn approbation. At this moment, the most trifling cause will produce the greatest effect: it is a spark which falls upon a mine of gunpowder.

A holy priest of the diocese of Amiens in France, named Peter; and from the solitary life he led, surnamed the hermit, tired of retirement, or prompted by the devotion of the times,

[11] Vertot, hist. de Malte.

BOOK
I.

quitted his cell , and wandered to Jerufalem. His mind fank within him, when, in the moments of fervent piety, he caft his eyes round, and faw the defolation of the holy places. With tears he lamented the circumftance to Simeon , the patriarch of the city, who in the zeal and character of his pilgrim foon difcovered difpofitions , from which poffibly great advantage might be drawn. They often met; and it was finally agreed between them, that Simeon fhould write a letter, defcriptive of the melancholy fituation of things, to the bifhop of Rome: this letter the hermit engaged to prefent, and to ftrengthen its contents by all the energy of his own reprefentation. He further promifed to vifit the courts of the European princes , and to roufe them, if poffible, to a general confederation for the relief of Jerufalem. Peter once more bent his knee at the holy fepulchre, and departed full of the great project, with which heaven , he thought, had infpired him. He prefented his difpatches to Urban , and as he had engaged , accompanied them with a pathetic detail of the horrors, his own eyes had witneffed. The effect anfwered his moft fanguine wifhes : Urban was affected , and on the fpot conceived the defign of fending relief to the chriftians of Paleftine. — Nor did the hermit delay the remaining part of his commiffion. He

travelled from court to court: was every where
received as a meffenger from heaven; and the
enthufiafm, he himfelf felt, was eafily transfufed
into the breafts of his hearers.

Peter was an engine admirably adapted to the
work he had undertaken. His zeal was ardent,
his difintereftednefs exemplary, and a fpirit of
mortification feemed to hold all his paffions
under the fevereft control. His figure, indeed,
was rather mean, and his phyfignomy unpleafant;
but his eye was piercing, and from his lips fell
a torrent of impaffioned eloquence, which
hurried his audience into admiration and conviction. He fpoke with the impofing air and
authority of an infpired man. The alms that
were given him he diftributed among the poor;
his food was dry bread, and he drank of the
chriftal ftream: his feet were bare, and a fingle
woollen tunic protected him from the inclemencies of various climes. And in all this, hiftorians
fay, there did not appear the leaft affectation.
Wherever he moved, crowds flocked to fee the
extraordinary man, and even he was deemed
happy who could procure a few hairs from the
faithful mule, the companion of his journeys
and his toils ".

In 1095 was affembled a council at Clermont in

" Daniel, Fleury.

Auvergne, at which Urban prefided in perfon.
Difturbances in Italy had compelled him to take
refuge in France. In this fynod was brought
forward the bufinefs of the holy land; the pope
addreffed them in a difcourfe full of pathetic
declamation and of fome good fenfe; and the
affembly, with enthufiafm, applauded the propofed undertaking, exclaiming with one voice,
deus lo volt, *it is the will of heaven.* The
pontiff feized the important moment. " The
" words you have uttered, faid he, were
" indeed dictated by heaven itfelf; I read
" infpiration in them and they fhall go with
" you into battle, to be your comfort and
" to be the fign, which fhall diftinguifh the
" true foldiers of the lord. " — He then
ordered that the figure of a *crofs* fhould be
borne on the breafts of thofe, who fhould
enrol themfelves in the facred warfare; and
ftill better to fecure fuccefs to his project,
(for he knew that enthufiafm was but a tran-
fient affection) he had recourfe to an expedient, which promifed to anfwer his warmeft
wifhes ".

At all times, fays the inimitable Fleury, whofe
reflections and ideas I am ever proud to copy,
the paftors of the church had ufed a difcretionary

" Daniel, Fleury.

power in the relaxation of fome parts of the canonical penances impofed on finners, as their fervor, or other circumftances, feemed to require it: but never, before this day, had it been feen that, for one fingle work of piety, a finner was difcharged from all the temporal punifhments, to which he might be liable before the juftice of heaven. Urban undertook to do as much as this, when he promifed a *plenary indulgence*, that is, a complete releafement from all temporal punifhment, to the crufaders. It was an innovation in the difcipline of the church, from which many abufes followed.—For more than two centuries, great difficulty had attended the enforcement of the penitentiary canons: In themfelves they were very fevere, and in procefs of time, fo much had they been multiplied, that almoft they might be deemed impracticable. From this circumftance arofe the difcipline of *commutation*, whereby whole years of penance might be redeemed in a few days. Pilgrimages to Rome, to Compoftella, to Jerufalem, entered into this fyftem of commutation; all which acts however were now left far behind by the new project of Urban, which to the meritorious exercife of a wandering life fuperadded the dreadful perils of war [s].

[s] Fleury, difc. 6.

In this firſt expedition, the cruſaders were uninfluenced by any ſordid motives: they looked for no ſalary, but what the papal indulgence held out to them.—Great certainly was the expenſe which attended the march of ſuch numerous armies; but the rich principally defrayed it, whilſt even the leſs wealthy contributed all they could procure, well knowing that the intereſt it would bring, was more highly to be prized than all human riches.—The ſagacious Urban imagined another device, which was no leſs efficacious. Under the ſevereſt cenſures, he forbad the cruſaders to be moleſted by their creditors, and granted them many other exemptions, whilſt they wore the holy croſs; and all their poſſeſſions, he took into the protection of the holy ſee.

Such favors would be received with ardor. The nobility feeling a load of crimes, from the pillage of churches, and a long ſeries of rapacity and oppreſſion, eagerly accepted ſuch eaſy terms of forgiveneſs: they had only to continue their favorite exerciſe of war, knowing that, if they fell, they ſhould receive the blooming palm of martyrdom".—The commonalty followed the example of their lords indeed, they were their vaſſals and bound to ſervitude: but when all that was great and elegant in the provinces was ſeen hurrying into arms, he muſt have been

" Fleury, ibid.

lowly-minded truly, who could have been contented to have flaid at home, bent over the anvil, or toiling behind his plough.

Churchmen, whofe pure hands fhould never be ftained with blood, were not excluded from this meritorious fervice. They alfo had crimes, which called for expiation, though in ftrictnefs of penitentiary difcipline, they were not fubject to its canons. In fome, motives of piety, but in more the love of novelty and diffipation, would preponderate.—Monks, with their abbots, broke from their retirement ; threw afide the cowl, and gliftened in the burnifhed helmet.— The fofter fex felt a glow of courage rife within their breafts, and they prepared to enter on the toilfome march, in company of their hufbands and their lovers.—Europe, in a word, was in general commotion : every eye fparkled with animation : in every town and in every village was heard the din of arms; whilft the crufader, leaning on his fword, uttered words of hardihood, talked of the battles he fhould win, and of the infidels he fhould maffacre, and of the fins which would be forgiven him. — In all the provinces of France, fays Daniel, private hoftilities ceafed in a moment, the moft inveterate enemies became friends ; and he that had not money ftrove to fell his poffeffions. The fcene was aftonifhing.

The principal crusaders were Hugh, brother to the French king; Robert duke of Normandy, brother to William Rufus of England ; Stephen count of Blois; Raymond count of Toulouse; Godfrey duke of Lorraine , with his brothers Baldwin and Eustach; with numberless inferior lords, knights , and gentlemen, bishops, abbots, monks, and priests.

By the beginning of 1096, the year after the council , the number of those, who had taken up the cross, was incredible. They assembled round Peter the hermit , whom they regarded as the apostle of the crusade, and as the envoy from heaven. From him they had their orders, and they prepared to march. — The first division, an undisciplined and lawless rabble, was led on by one Walter, a French gentleman of some experience, but of little note. He was followed by the hermit, at the head of forty thousand men. A third division of fifteen thousand proceeded under Gotescale, a German priest. — Great were the disorders these men committed ; the latter division in particular ; against whom the insulted people of Hungary rose up in arms, and it is said, not one of the fifteen thousand survived to tell the tale of their catastrophe. — Other bands, still more numerous, followed in wonderful succession, and as their excesses on the march were as great, many of them shared the just fate of their fellows ".

" Daniel, Vertot.

A more undifciplined and licentious body of men never drew the fword. In truth, there was but little difcipline in the armies of the age, and in thofe of the crufaders there was ftill lefs: they were formed of volunteers from different nations, the chief over whom were independent of one another, and as lawlefs and licentious as they. ·The pope's legate alone held fupreme command, and his voice, it was vainly expected, would awe into obedience this difcordant multitude. Impatient of control, they waited not till they fhould have put their feet on infidel land, to commence hoftilities; wherever they marched, pillage, rapine, devaftation marked their progrefs. They had, indeed, been vainly taught to believe, that heaven, by fupernatural affiftance, would fupply all their neceffities, and therefore no provifion had been made for fubfiftence on the march. Finding their wild expectations fruftrated, they were even compelled to relieve their wants by plunder; and this it was that enraged the inhabitants of the countries through which they paffed. They took their way towards Conftantinople, through Hungary and Bulgaria.

The princes, whofe names I have mentioned, apprehenfive probably left the greatnefs itfelf of the armament fhould difappoint its own purpofe, permitted the multitude to march before them, and themfelves, by different routes, efcorted by the flower of their vaffals, advanced towards the feat of the Eaftern empire; for that was appointed the place of general rendezvous.

Alexis Comnenus, the Greek emperor, faw them approach with difmay. He had applied indeed to the Weftern chriftians for fuccour againft the Turks, but he had only hoped that fuch a fupply would be fent him, as, acting under his control, might enable him to repel the enemy. Aftonifhed he was to fee his dominions overwhelmed, on a fudden, by fuch an inundation of licentious barbarians, who, though they pretended friendfhip, defpifed his fubjects as unwarlike, and detefted them as heretical. By all the arts of policy, in which he excelled, he endeavoured to divert the torrent; but while he employed profeffions, careffes, civilities, and feeming fervices towards the leaders of the crufade, he fecretly regarded thofe imperious allies as more dangerous than the open enemies, by whom his empire had been Invaded. Whilft the armies were round his capital he daily haraffed them by every art, which his genius, his power, or his fituation enabled him to employ; and having effected the difficult point of difembarking them in Afia, he entered into a private corref-

pondence

pondence with Soliman, the Turkish emperor, and he practised every infidious device, for difappointing the enterprife, and difcouraging the latins from attempting thenceforward any fuch prodigious migrations.

On the banks of the Bofphorus, oppofite to Conftantinople, the generals reviewed their armies, when the number of men was found to amount to one hundred thoufand horfe, and fix hundred thoufand foot, including all the attendants of the army. —The advanced parties, under Walter and the hermit, who had imprudently penetrated into the heart of the country, were foon overpowered, and cut to pieces. Peter was abfent at Conftantinople. — The grand army proceeded on their enterprife with more circumfpection : but the fcarcity of provifions, the exceffes of fatigue, the influence of unexperienced climates, joined to the want of concert in their operations, and to the fword of a warlike enemy, deftroyed the adventurers by thoufands. Their zeal, however, their bravery, and their irrefiftible force ftill carried them forward. — After an obftinate fiege, Niĉe, the feat of the Turkifh empire, fell; they defeated Soliman in two great battles, and they fat down before Antioch. After various events, Antioch alfo furrendered, and the force of the enemy, who till now had proudly refifted, feemed entirely broke.

Flufhed with fuccefs, the champions of the crofs advanced towards Jerufalem, which they regarded as the confummation of their labors. By the detachments they had made to fecure their conquefts, by defertion, and by difafters, their number was reduced to twenty thoufand foot, and fifteen hundred horfe; but thefe were ftill formidable, from their valor, their experience, and the obedience which, from paft calamities, they had learned to pay to their leaders. — From the heights which command Jerufalem, they looked down on the holy city, their hearts beat for joy, they forgot their labors, and they demanded, in clamorous fhouts, to be led up to the walls, though they were defended by an army of forty thoufand men.

In formidable preparation, the generals took their pofts round the devoted city; Godfrey of Bouillon, Robert of Normandy, Raymond of Touloufe, Robert of Flanders, and the valiant Tancred. Their refolution was unanimous, to die, or to conquer. Nor was the enemy within the walls lefs prepared or lefs determined. The fiege lafted five weeks, during which, feats of heroifm were achieved, which hiftorians and poets have been careful to record and to magnify. A general affault was finally projected, and with the rifing fun the trumpet founded. It was Friday, the

15th of July, in 1099, till an hour after mid-day, with infinite refolution, the affailants maintained their pofts, and the befieged refifted. But human ftrength could do no more, and Godfrey faw in the countenances of his men, that they defpaired of fuccefs. They panfed; when, on a fudden, the voice of their general founded in their ears: " My friends , cried he, heaven is for us; fee " yonder the clouds open, and an armed warrior " defcends upon the mountain of Olives ; his " fhield darts lightning, and he beckons to us to " advance!"—Raymond of Touloufe faw the fame vifion. " It is St. George, faid he, and he calls " us to victory."—In a moment every arm was again braced ; they reared their ladders , their rams fhook the walls , their machines advanced, and Godfrey, fword in hand, was feen upon the ramparts, furrounded by his brave companions. The enemy gave way on all fides , and on all fides entered the victorious champions of the crofs.

The carnage and fcenes of horror, which now enfued, were, paft defcription, dreadful. Imagination itfelf is loft in the painful image, and recoils. Neither arms defended the valiant, nor fubmiffion the timorous: no age or fex was fpared. The ftreets of Jerufalem were covered with dead bodies. — But the triumphant warriors, after every enemy was

fubdued and flaughtered, immediately turned
themfelves, with fentiments of humiliation and
contrition, towards the holy fepulchre. Without
quitting their bloody armour, they advanced
with reclined bodies, and with naked feet, to
that facred monument. They were met, with
hymns of jubilation, by the chriflians they had
refcued, and with them they fang anthems to
their Saviour, who had there purchafed their
falvation by his agony and death. Enlivened by
the prefence of the place, devotion fo overcame
all their martial fury, that they diffolved in tears,
and bore the appearance of every foft and
tender fentiment. So inconfiflent is human nature
with itfelf! and fo eafily do all the paffions ally,
fuperftition efpecially and enthufiafm, with heroic
courage, and fierce barbarity!

Eight days after this great event, Godfrey of
Bouillon was unanimoufly chofen king of Jerufalem. Among all the warriors he was the moft
eminent: courage, wifdom, martial fkill, probity,
religion, prudence, flrength of body, and a flature
which awed the beholder, marked him for a hero,
and united all the fuffrages in his favor. For
one year only he held this romantic fceptre with
a dignity, which the hand of Godfrey alone could
have given to it: he died, and was lamented. —
The other princes, having performed their vows
returned in hafte to Europe, where neglected

vaſſals, and the important concerns of ſtate, had long bewailed their abſence ".

Thus ended the firſt cruſade. — In whatever light it be conſidered, whether as an objeﬄ of religion or of policy, I can diſcover no one permanent advantage that was derived from it. Jeruſalem, indeed, was taken; the chriſtian inhabitants would be proteﬄed, and future pilgrims would approach the holy places in more ſecurity. To the ſuperſtition of the age theſe might be weighty benefits; and who will ſay that, as ſuch, they might not value them? Still their greateſt advantages, it ſeems, ſhould vaniſh, when contraſted with their concomitants, the direful events of war. But this alſo is a reflexion to which, I know not, that the chriſtians of the eleventh century would have ſubſcribed.

From a redundancy of population, as Europe then was circumſtanced, had, in great meaſure, ariſen that exceſs of vice and lawleſs diſſipation, which I deſcribed; and it was natural to imagine that the vaſt armies which marched to the Eaſt would be principally compoſed of the refuſe of ſociety: hence would the community at large be benefited. — So it happened, and not one, in a hundred ever ſaw again his native land; but this one, together with the vices he had taken with

" Vertot, Fleury, Daniel, Hume, from original authors.

F 3

BOOK I.

him, returned loaded with all thofe which the Eaftern nations were beft able to fupply. On the other hand, was the lofs of fo many brave, honeft, and virtuous man, who fell facrifice to the phrenzy of the times, to weigh as nothing in the fcale of reafon? — The inteftine feuds, indeed, which fo long had defolated Europe, ceafed, for a moment, in their dread career, while the blood of infidels was pouring out round the walls of Jerufalem : but foon they refumed their wonted fury, and raged as before.

Afia was then the feat of the arts, of learning, and of commerce; and from thence, in procefs of time, Europe was to draw the moft fubftantial benefits. In the firft crufade thefe were not perceptible; nor could they be: but a channel, it muft be owned, was then opened, through which, in a ftream at firft but fmall, they might begin to flow towards the Weftern world. The politicians of the age had not this object, I believe, in view: but is it from the forefight of man or not rather from what appears to us a fortuitous concurrence of circumftances, that the moft fubftantial advantages have been derived on human kind?

END OF THE FIRST BOOK.

THE

HISTORY

OF THE LIVES OF

ABEILLARD and HELOISA.

BOOK II.

*Abeillard goes to Laon and studies under Anselm —
Returns to Paris and teaches. — Heloifa —Abeillard
becomes her mafter — She efcapes with him into
Britany — He offers to marry her — They are married — He conveys her to Argenteuil — Fulbert's
revenge — Pafcal II. pope of Rome — France and
England — Religious orders — Cluni — The Chartreufe — Fontevraud.*

Anno, 1100.

FROM the contentious fcenes of war and politics, on which the pride of hiftory loves to dwell, I return, with pleafure, to the more humble walk of biography. Thus the traveller, who, on the glacieres of Grindelwald or Chamoigny, has contemplated nature in her fublimeft horrors, finks to

F 4

BOOK
II.
the vale below with gentler emotions, where he meets the creeping woodbine and the purling ftream.

He goes to
Laon and
ftudies under
Anfelm.
The reader will recollect that he left Abeillard, juft returned from Britany to Paris, rather difgufted of philofophical purfuits , and preparing to enter on the more important ftudy of theology. His old mafter and competitor de Champeaux , elated with the new honors of the mitre, had withdrawn to Chalons.

Laon , an epifcopal fee , diftant twenty-feven leagues from Paris , was at this time celebrated for its chair of divinity. There Anfelm, a canon and dean of the chapter, had for many years taught, with the greateft applaufe: men of the firft confequence in the church had been his fcholars[1]. In this number muft be reckoned de Champeaux himfelf. Abeillard looking round for a mafter, from whom he might draw fome inftruction in the new purfuit he was meditating, naturally fixed on Anfelm. Independently of other confiderations, the circumftance of his having taught the bifhop of Chalons, would have fome weight on his mind. The man we contend with , and conquer, is feldom deemed a contemptible antagonift. — He went to Laon.

" I frequented, fays he, the old man's fchool, " but it was foon evident, that all his celebrity was

[1] Notæ ad hift. Cal.

" derived, not from the difplay of abilities, but
" from length of practice. He who approached.
" him in anxious uncertainty, returned in a
" thicker cloud. To hear him was delightful;
" for he poffeffed an aftonifhing fluency of lan-
" guage; but in his words was neither reafon nor
" common fenfe. You would have thought he
" were kindling a fire, when inftantly the whole
" houfe was filled with fmoke, in which not a
" fingle fpark was vifible. He was a tree, covered
" with a thick foliage, which to the diftant eye
" had charms; but on a nearer infpection there
" was no fruit to be found. I went up to this
" tree in full expectation: my eye beheld that it
" was the fig-tree, which the Lord had curfed;
" or I faid it might be the oak with which the
" poet compares Pompey,

" Stat magni nominis umbra ,
" Qualis frugifero quercus fublimis in agro.
" Lucan. Phar.

" And after this difcovery, I repofed not many
" days under its noxious fhade '."
The portrait is ftrongly taken, but refentment
probably preffed on the pencil in the darker
coloring.
Of this fame Anfelm a curious anecdote is told
by an old author ', which, as it may ferve to

* Hift. Cal.   ' Notæ ad hift. Cal.

mark the character of the age, I fhall relate. —
A confiderable part of the gold and jewels, belonging to the church of Laon, had been ftolen. The
thief could not be difcovered; whereupon a general meeting of the canons and principal citizens
was called. Uncertain what to do, they unanimoufly
agreed to take the opinion of Anfelm, who was
efteemed the oracle of the town. Anfelm, deeply
verfed in the law and prophets, revolves the whole
bufinefs in his mind, and recollects at laft the
paffage in the book of Jofhua, where it is related,
in what manner, a fecret theft had been detected
by the cafting of lots. " It is my advice, faid
" he, having weighed the matter moft deliberately,
" that you try to difcover the author of this horrid
" crime by the *ordeal* of water. Let an infant be
" taken from each parifh, and caft into a veffel
" of holy water: from the child which finks, will
" the guilty parifh be known. Then from each
" houfe of this parifh take another infant: which
" will fhow you the guilty houfe. You can be no
" longer at a lofs: throw every man and woman
" belonging to the houfe into tubs of holy water,
" and guilt will be concealed no longer." The
experiment, I prefume, fucceeded; for the fame
author relates that the thief was a perfon, by name
alfo Anfelm, who, under the cloak of extraordinary piety, had impofed on many, and to whofe
care had been intrufted the rich ornaments of
the church.

Abeillard, whom the emptinefs of this wordy veteran could not fail to difguft, began to appear lefs frequently at his lectures. It was a more prudent ftep, than to have attempted a direct attack on the great name of his mafter. Age had given fome check to the petulancy of his temper, or by experience he had learned wifdom. His abfence however from the fchools was foon noticed; it was conftrued by thofe, among the fcholars, who plumed themfelves moft on their abilities, into a reflection on their own difcernment. He dares to undervalue the great Anfelm, faid they. The old man was himfelf irritable and jealous : he had inftructed the brighteft geniufes of the age, and been admired by them: was this child of Ariftotle alone to withhold his applaufe, juft as his fun, with its full effulgence, was fetting in the Weft! The fuggeftions of the young men, whofe pride was alfo piqued, only ferved to fan into a wilder flame the indignation of the old profeffor [*].

It happened that, as one day the fcholars were jokingly converfing together, one of them afked Abeillard, what he thought about the ftudy of the fcriptures? The queftion was captious, as they well knew, how little attention he had hitherto given to thofe divine books. He replied that, if religious improvement be the object, no ftudy

[*] Hift. Calam.

certainly was so salutary; but added that, to him it was matter of great surprise, how any one, who had the smallest pretensions to literature, could possibly imagine that, besides the scriptures themselves and some easy expositor, any other assistance should be deemed necessary to render them most perfectly intelligible. — The proposition was received with scorn, and insultingly they asked Abeillard, whether he perhaps might think himself equal to the undertaking. "I am ready to "do it, said he; chuse what book, you please, "from the old or new testament, one that is "rarely explained in the schools, and with it allow me but a single commentator. "—It was instantly agreed to; and they fixed on the prophecy of Ezekiel [1].

The next morning he acquainted the young men, that he was prepared to fulfil his engagement. His friends advised him to be less precipitate; they told him he was a novice in theology; and that he should proceed, in so arduous an undertaking, with the greatest circumspection and leisure. "It is not by leisure, answered he angrily, "but by energy of genius, that I pretend to "master the great heights of science: either I "will be heard when, and in what manner, "it pleases me best, or, this moment, I am free from my engagement. "

[1] Hist. Calam.

But few were prefent at the firft lecture: the attempt was deemed both arrogant and ridiculous. He acquitted himfelf, however, fo much to the fatisfaction of his hearers, that they requefted he would proceed, and they complimented him on the precifion and fublimity of his comment. The following days, the whole town preffed to hear him; every word he uttered was carefully taken down; and, as it had before happened at Melun and Paris, the ftreets of Laon echoed with the name of Abeillard [*].

The found foon reached the ears of Anfelm. His mind, for fome days, had been cruelly on the fret: this youth, whofe hours in the ftudy of divinity hardly meafured his years of practice, in one fingle night, had penetrated into the obfcure myfteries of Ezekiel, and had drawn that veil afide, which himfelf perhaps had not dared to touch. The circumftance was infulting, and he vowed revenge. But though pious minds can be fometimes fwayed by the paffions of finners, they are wonderfully adroit at the difcovery of motives, which, to their own eyes, at leaft, may fanctify their proceedings.

Anfelm had, amongft his fchólars, two, whom he particularly efteemed, and whofe abilities were fuperior to the reft, Albericus, a native of Rheims, and Lotulphus, from Novara in Lombardy; which

[*] Hift. Calam.

place however was rendered far more famous for giving birth to Peter bishop of Paris, the celebrated *master of sentences*. These men, buoyed up by a sense of their own superiority and the flattering approbation of Anselm, would feel more poignantly the burst of applause, which, in a moment, had raised Abeillard far above them. It was their advice, that the expositor of Ezekiel should be interdicted from proceeding any further in his public comment. — The old man acceded joyfully to their proposal. He alone was theologal in Laon, and without his permission no one could be empowered to give lectures. The prohibition was notified to Abeillard, under this pretext that, should any error, peradventure, creep into the exposition of the prophecy, which, (from his inexperience in theology, might too easily happen) the whole blame would be imputed to Anselm; that he could not expose the whole glory of a well-earned reputation upon so slippery a surface; and that religion, in a secret whisper, had told him to be circumspect.

The scholars, who patronised Abeillard, heard the news of this event with indignation; the thin veil which covered the real motives of Anselm's conduct was easily penetrated; but all opposition, they saw, would be vain. Abeillard resolved to withdraw; Laon was not a theatre wide enough for the display of his abilities, and the grey hairs of the theologal called for some respect. Anselm triumphed in his fuccefs; even the day, on which, by his conjuring fagacity, he had proved his name-fake to be a facrilegious robber, was not half fo glorious [1].

As the memoirs, from which the ftory of the life of Abeillard is principally drawn, were written by himfelf, and that after, by a feries of misfortunes and ill-ufage, he had been feverely irritated, fome allowance fhould be made for partial narration. For however little difpofed he might really be to depart from truth, it is too obvious, that objects take their tinge from the complexion of our own minds. In an inftant how changed is the fcene, when to the varied beauties of the rifing fun fucceed murky clouds and a lowering fky! It muft alfo be confeffed that the conduct of the young man was often reprehenfible. His abilities were of a fuperior caft, and he was gifted with a penetration, which at once laid open to his eye the whole texture of character: from this he felected the weakeft parts, and he took a malignant pleafure in exhibiting them to public view. Such a man could hardly have a friend, for he feemed to have no indulgence for the weakneffes of human nature. Himfelf had not yet experienced how low the greateft minds may fink. Unremittingly he had purfued the object of his ambition, and this was of a nature only to draw into action thofe

[1] Hift. Calam.

powers of his foul, which were pure and intellectual. From this circumftance he would deem highly of himfelf, and viewing others in the fame medium, them naturally he might defpife. The judgment of youth is often erroneous.

Abeillard once more returned to Paris. Fame had not been filent during his refidence at Laon; it was known with what fplendor he had opened his new career; theology had woven a garland to encircle his brows; his friends were waiting to receive him: and the doors of the fchools ftood open. He began his lectures with the prophecy of Ezekiel, completing the expofition he had commenced in the country. His auditors were charmed; the firft philofopher, they faid, was become the furft divine. Multitudes of frefh fcholars flowed in from all quarters: he therefore judged proper to refume his old lecture of philofophy [*]. The fifter fciences were pleafed with this amiable union; they had too long been kept afunder from each other; and both from the mouth of Abeillard received new ftrength and new charms.

In the following words does a contemporary fpeak of thefe times in a letter addrelled to Abeillard: " No diftance of country, no height " of mountains, no depth of vallies, no intricate " journey befet with perils and thieves, could with- " hold your fcholars from you. Rome fent her
                                        " children

[*] Hift. Calam.

" children to receive your inſtruction: ſhe who had
" been the miſtreſs of every ſcience now confeſſed
" her inferiority. The youth of Britain crowding
" to their ſhores were not intimidated by the ſea
" which met their eyes, or the billows that broke
" at their feet: in ſpite of danger, they cleared
" the dreadful paſs. The more remote iſlands
" diſmiſſed their ſavage ſons. Germany, Spain,
" Flanders, the people of the North and of the
" South, flocked to you; in their mouths your
" name only was heard ; they admired, they
" praiſed, they extolled your abilities. I ſpeak
" not of thoſe whom the walls of Paris encloſed,
" nor of the inhabitants of our neighbouring or
" more diſtant provinces: from you they as ardently
" ſought for wiſdom, as if all its treaſures had been
" there locked up. In a word, moved by the
" ſplendor of your genius, by the charms of your
" elocution, and by the acuteneſs of your penetra-
" tion, to you they all approached, as to the
" ſource from which ſcience flowed in the pureſt
" ſtream * "

But the theology of the times conſiſted in little
elſe than a bare expoſition of ſcripture-paſſages;
a method however, by which, had it been
purſued in a cool and rational manner, religion
might have gained much. It would not have
been loaded with that ſuperfluity of idle matter,

---

* Fulco ad Abeil. p. 218.

which has disfigured its native simplicity; and to
which an undue importance has ever been given.
The commentators of the twelfth century were
not satisfied with a plain and literal explanation
of the text : they thought that, under each line,
lay something of a spiritual or myftical meaning,
and of this they were ever in queft. It was the
bad tafte of the age, to which unadorned simplicity could give no pleafure: or elfe the literal
fenfe was to their apprehenfion peculiarly difficult,
from their ignorance of the primitive languages,
in which the books of fcripture were written;
and becaufe they knew fo little of the hiftory and
of the 'manners of ancient times. What we do
not underfland is the more fufceptible of a myftic
interpretation, and rather than own our ignorance,
what abfurdities will not be advanced "?

From the licentioufnefs of allegorical expofition
any maxims might be drawn. They read in the
gofpel of St. Luke, that our Saviour, before his
pafiion, told his difciples, that fwords would be
neceffary : they anfwered, behold here are two
fwords. He replied; it is enough. — The fenfe
of this paffage is obvious; but commentators
difcovered that, by the two fwords were fignified
the fpiritual and temporal powers, by which the
world is governed ; and that thefe powers
belonged both to the church , becaufe the
two fwords were in the hands of the apoftles.

" Fleury , dif. 5.

The church indeed, they faid, fhould herfelf only exercife the fpiritual power, and intruft the other to the prince. Our faviour faid to Peter; put up thy fword into the fcabbard; that is, the fword, Peter, is thine; but it is not in thy hand it fhould be ufed; give it to the Prince, who fhall employ it, as thou fhalt order and direct". — On fuch deductions as thefe was grounded the depofing doctrine of Rome, and all the vain fuperftructure of prerogative and privilege, which the church exercifed, with an unbounded fway, through the long period of many years.

·In the full blow of literary honors, which the breath of envy did not attempt to blaft, and fecure in the applaufe of an admiring public, the days of Abeillard now flowed on in one unruffled ftream. The fame tide brought wealth and glory with it. But as rivalry and oppofition ceafed, fo, on his fide ceafed thofe vigorous exertions, which had made him what he was. The nervous fyftem; I have elfewhere obferved, upon the tone of which all our animation depends, foon relaxes, when the fpur is withdrawn that excited its vibrations; and when this happens, a languor enfues, with which the whole man fympathizes in wonderful accord. — Affections began to rife, to which hitherto he had been a ftranger and he found he was not that hero, which, in vanity of mind, he had once imagined.

G 2

" Fleury, difc. 5.

Even Hercules, in the gay court of Omphale, threw down his club, and submitted to hold the distaff.

Paris was, at this time, a scene of general dissipation: it was so, as the principal residence of the French court, and as an academy crowded with the youth of different nations. No discipline could have held such an unruly multitude in control. The description, which historians give of the vice and depravity of the scholars, can only. be conceived by viewing modern seminaries of learning. — Abeillard, in the midst of this alluring scene, would hardly withstand its fascination. He was young, handsome, agreeable. The splendor of his public character, as it drew on him the . eye of admiration, so was it a passport, which admitted him into the first circles of Paris. His company was eagerly sought for: he charmed in conversation; the tone of his voice was melodious; he sang well, and his songs were often pieces of his own composition [11].

Speaking of himself at this period, he says: " It " is in the lap of prosperity that the mind swells " with foolish vanity; its vigor is enervated by " repose, while the indulgence of pleasure " completes the victory. At a time, when I " thought myself the first philosopher in Europe, " nor feared to be disturbed in my seat of " eminence, then it was, that I who had " been a pattern of virtue, first loosened the

[11] Ep. Helois. 1ª.

" rein at the call of paffion. In proportion as
" I ha.; rifen higher on the fcale of literary
" excellence, the lower did I fink into vicious
" depravity. I quitted thofe paths of virtue,
" which all my predeceffors had trodden with
" fo much renown. Pride and pleafure were the
" monfters that fubdued me ". " — In this
fituation of undifturbed repofe, of diffipation, and
of honor, Abeillard had paffed near five years,
extolled as the firft mafter of the age, courted
by the great, loved by the gay, feared by the
ignorant, and admired by all.

There was then in Paris a young lady, of great
beauty, but whom her talents and extraordinary
advance in fcience, rendered an object of general
admiration. She was in the richeft bloom of
youth, having reached her eighteenth year ";
a period, when the mind, if properly cultivated,
begins to expand on the countenance, and to
give it an expreffion which it had not before
Heloifa, for this was the young lady's name,
lived with her uncle Fulbert, a canon of the
cathedral church. — By fome fhe is faid to have
been defcended from the illuftrious houfe of
Montmorency; whilft others pretend, fhe was
the natural daughter of a prieft ". — Be this as
it may; nature had formed her of her beft
materials, and fhe was the darling of her uncle.

" Hift. Calam. " Vie d'Abeil. p. 48. " Bayle, letter H.

The old man had spared no expense in the education of his niece. In other regards niggardly, here he was profuse; and whatever, in the literary arts of the age, the best masters had to give, that he endeavoured to procure for Heloisa. — She is represented as a prodigy in science: but it should seem as if her encomiasts, willing to delineate a phenomenon in the female world, had brought together every excellence their minds could fancy, and had presented the rich gift to the niece of Fulbert. It was not only in the circles of Paris, they say, that her name was familiar: It had penetrated to the extreme parts of the kingdom [11]. — When learning is possessed by few, a very ordinary portion is viewed with admiration. We may judge by comparison; and can it be presumed that, in the gloomy era of the twelfth century, even to Heloisa science would have unlocked those treasures, which the female candidates of modern times would perhaps ask of her in vain? She was acquainted, it is said, with the best authors of ancient Rome, had been deeply initiated in the philosophy of the age, and knew what the wise men of antiquity had taught. The Latin and Greek languages were familiar to her, and even rising from the cradle, she had been heard to lisp the psalms of David, in the very language of their royal author [12]. — When retirement and the appli-

[11] Prev. Apologet.   [12] Ibid.

cation of maturer years had given full improvement to her mind; I doubt not, but she became
poſſeſſed of all theſe high accompliſhments, which
at the age of eighteen, the generoſity of antici-
pation ſeems to have beſtowed upon her. — She
was born in the firſt or ſecond year of the century.

Abeillard, though become a man of pleaſure,
had not loſt that delicacy of mind, which is
ſometimes ſo conſtitutional, as to remain with us
even in the abſence of virtue. He had ever deteſted
low vice, and the company of abandoned women
was peculiarly odious to him [1]. Public diſſipation
was incompatible with the dignity of his ſtation;
nor could his attendance on the ſchools permit
him to frequent the ſociety of thoſe ladies, who
would not, he thinks, have been inſenſible to the
charms of his perſon and converſation.

It was at this moment of ſelf-complacency and
enervation, that began his acquaintance with the
accompliſhed Heloiſa. The houſe, where her uncle
reſided, was contiguous to the public ſchools.
Doubtleſs he had often ſeen her, and often heard
of her uncommon abilities; but till now ſuch
objects were little calculated to make a ſenſible
impreſſion. In the retired ſituation and amiable
qualities of this young lady, he ſoon diſcovered
all that his heart could wiſh for. That he himſelf
was irreſiſtible, he had the fulleſt conviction. "So

[1] Hiſt. Calam.

G 4

" great, fays he, was my reputation, and fo
" captivating the attractions of my youth and
" perfon, that I feared not to be rejected by any
" woman, whom I fhould deign to honor with
" my regard." Yet was not this vain philofopher
very diftant from his fortieth year.

Befides thefe perfonal attractions, there were
other circumftances, which might feem no lefs
flattering. He well knew the progrefs Heloifa had
made in learning, and how warmly her foul was
engaged in the purfuit. Could he draw her into
a correfpondence of letters, (a propofal which he
doubted not fhe would embrace with ardor,)
he forefaw every fuccefs in the event. Then he
could flatter her vanity with lefs danger of fufpicion: he could, with more freedom and in ftrong-
er colors, exprefs the emotions of his heart; and
though her company might be fometimes denied
him, he could by this intercourfe, at leaft, keep
alive the impreffion on her mind". The plan
was concerted. — But it is not faid how long this
correfpondence lafted, nor is it faid, whether he
was admitted to any private interview with her.
Heloifa would be delighted by the marked attention of this great man; nor from inexperience and
from the high opinion fhe had of him, could fhe,
for a moment, fufpect his intentions. Abeillard muft
have recoiled when he viewed the infamy of his
defign : it could not poffibly be that, at once, he

" Hift. Calam.

should embark in a fixed scheme of seduction. He says it however himself in words which cannot be mistaken [20]; and if so, he must be pronounced a much worse man, than otherwise I could be disposed to believe him. In the high regions of romantic speculation he had lost sight of, or never known, those amiable virtues, without which the greatest talents may be deemed a curse from the hand of providence.

Warmed by acquaintance and the intercourse of sentiment, to which the unguarded innocence of Heloisa would give additional charms, the affections of Abeillard grew into passion. He that should have been her friend, became her lover; and the reserve and distant correspondence, he had hitherto maintained, could satisfy no longer. He meditated other schemes; but, had his intentions been honorable, where was the necessity of disguise? Fulbert would have opened his doors, and have been proud in the society of Abeillard.

The philosopher well imagined, that the respect, produced by the great celebrity of his name, with which the young lady received his addresses, would gradually wear down into a more familiar behaviour, could he have the happiness of seeing her, and of conversing with her more frequently [21]; and his invention hit on a scheme, which proved him a finished master in the art of seduction. — He began to show great attention to some of Fulbert's

[20] Hist. Calam.   [21] Ibid.

friends; and when he thought them fecure, he opened to them his wifhes, which were, that they would propofe to the good man to take him into his houfe as a boarder. Its being fo near to the fchools, he faid, would be a great conveniency; that he fhould not hefitate upon terms, however high they might be; that the buftle and folicitude, neceffarily attendant on houfe-keeping, deranged that equanimity, which fludy called for; and that his expenfes were heavier than he could conveniently fupport. Fulbert, he knew, was very fond of money; and as the firft of his defires was to procure for his niece every means for her further improvement, he trufted, that his propofal, coming in fo eligible a form, would not be rejected[*]. — The old canon fwallowed the bait with eagernefs. Money, and with it the profpect of benefiting Heloifa, accorded with all the feelings of his heart. It was no trifling circumftance neither, that Abeillard fhould put his foot over his threfhold, and that he fhould be permitted to fit down at table with a man, whom the world admired. Thus vanity, which never dies in the human breaft, hung her bias alfo on the fide of his ruling paffions.

Of Fulbert an anecdote is recorded, which proves his piety to have been equal to his affection for money and for Heloifa. — The almoner of Henry, the French king, inftigated by an inordinate devo-

[*] Hift. Calam.

tion, had ftolen from the chapel of his mafter,
a large portion of the back-bone of Saint Ebrulfus.
Among the firft friends of this thief was canon
Fulbert, and to prove to him the excefs of his
love, he made him a prefent of what he efteemed
deareft in the world, this holy relic. Fulbert had
had it long in his poffeffion, when hearing probably by what iniquitous means it had been
procured, he feared to detain it any longer. He
affembled his friends, propofed the important
bufinefs, and earneftly befought their advice.
They agreed the back bone had been ftolen, and
could not with a fafe confcience be kept; the prior
of a neighbouring convent was therefore fent for;
to him was committed the facred treafure with
injunction, that he fhould forthwith convey it,
my author fays, to Utica, but I fuppofe to the
chapel from whence it had been taken. This at
leaft the principle of reftitution fhould have
fuggefted ".

When Abeillard had obtained the old-man's
permiffion to remove to his houfe, the firft thing
the latter propofed to him was, that he would
take fome charge of his niece. The philofopher
affented. That he would dedicate much of his
time to her inftruction, feemed an unreafonable
requeft: finally, however, he entreated him that,
fhould he have any vacant moments after his
return from fchool, either by night or day, them-

" Oderic. l. -. Hift. E.cl.

he would give to Heloifa; and ftill to evince how
much he prized his inftruction, it was his requeft,
he faid, that fhould he find her negligent or inattentive, he would chaftife her feverely. .

" Viewing this fimplicity of the uncle, I was
" not lefs aftonifhed, obferves Abeillard, than if I
" had beheld a fhepherd intrufting his lamb to the
" care of a hungry wolf. He committed his niece
" to me, to be taught, and to be corrected, as
" I pleafed ; which, in fact, was fupplying me
" with every occafion, not only of gaining her
" affections, but likewife with a power of forcing
" her, by chaftifement, to comply with my de-
" fires, fhould perfuafion prove ineffectual. But
" there were two confiderations, with which all
" fufpicion of evil was incompatible; the love he
" felt for Heloifa, and the opinion he entertained
" of my virtue". " — The bafe feducer felt not
himfelf the weight of thefe motives. Fulbert might
have been fimple; but it was a fimplicity which
did honor to his heart. Sufpicion never dwells
in an honeft mind. I am almoft tempted to
believe that the ftigma of covetoufnefs had been
fixed on Fulbert by the hand of inveterate
refentment.

The agitation and joy of mind, felt by Heloifa,
when fhe heard who the ftranger was that was
coming to refide under her uncle's roof, will
be eafily conceived. To the high opinion fame

" Hift. Cal.

had long impreffed on her mind, was now joined a more intimate acquaintance with the man; fhe had converfed with him, and fhe had received letters from his hand, at once expreffive of affection and of the idea he entertained of her abilities. This Abeillard was now to be her mafter, and fhe was to enjoy his fociety in the eafe of domeflic intercourfe. For an inftant, fhe could not fufpect him capable of any interefted or infidious views: fuch thoughts are, at leaft, inconfiftent with the candid innocence of youth. She faw him arrive with fuch emotions, as, the flate of mind I have defcribed, would naturally raife; but the moment, which Heloifa viewed as the brighteft of her life, was, in fact, clouded with the lowering decrees of late!

As the bafe defigns of Abeillard had been ma- turely projected, he would proceed to their accomplifhment by all thofe means which circum-ftances offered, and with an artifice, that well knew how to avail itfelf of the moft trifling incident. The fagacious logician who had foiled the firft mafters of the art, at their own weapons, now entered the lifts with a girl of eighteen: it was a noble conteft! — The gradations from refpect to love, through all their intermediate fhades, would be fenfibly marked on the foul of Heloifa, and Abeillard would read them on her counte-nance. — He very minutely, and with little delicacy, details the circumftances of their ftudious hours, and he tells the progrefs his pupil foon made in the art of love[14]. Indeed, the moft tried virtue could not have withflood this powerful ordeaL Heloifa began to love; and from a combination of incidents, joined to a natural caft of difpofitions, fuch a ftrength of paffion took poffeffion of her foul, as the wild annals of romance have never, I believe, equalled.

Abeillard now loft all relifh for the fchools; Ariftotle and fcripture-comments could pleafe no longer. His leffons were but a repetition of what he had faid before, and even thefe were delivered with an indifference, a precipitancy, and a vifible abfence of mind, which fhowed that his attention was engaged on other objects[15]. — His genius, however, was not abfolutely idle. As he often quotes the Latin poets, it is probable that he took delight in their compofitions: I have alfo already remarked, that he was not himfelf without fome pretenfions to poetry. Whatever talents he might have, the prefent moment would be fure to call them into play. Love makes poets of us all. For, as the feat of that paffion lies chiefly in the imagination, it is natural that thofe ideas fhould pleafe beft, which are in unifon with it. Abfent from Heloifa, his employment was to celebrate her praifes: he compofed fonnets, laid his fonnets at her feet, and he fang them to the tendereft airs[16].

[14] Hift. Calam.   [15] Ibid.   [16] Ep. Cal. Ep. Helois. 1[a].

Many years after, thus does Heloifa fpeak of thefe times, of Abeillard, and of his compofitions: warm with the recollection fhe fays to him: " You " poffeffed, Abeillard, two qualifications, a tone " of voice and a grace in finging, which gave " you the control over every female heart. " Thefe powers were peculiarly yours ; for I know " not that they ever fell to the lot of any other " philofopher. To foften, by playful amufement, " the ftern labors of philofophy, you compofed " feveral fonnets on love and on fimilar fubjects. " Thefe you were often heard to fing, when the " harmony of your voice gave new charms to " the beauty of your language. In all circles only " Abeillard was talked of: even the moft ignorant, " who could not judge of compofition, were " enchanted by the melody of your voice. Female " hearts could not withftand the impreffion. " Thus was my name foon carried to diftant " nations, for our loves were the theme of all " your fongs. Women envied my happinefs: they " faw you were endowed with every accomplifh- " ment of mind and body ". "

Thefe poems, as they were handed about, and continued to be very fafhionable fongs, even in countries remote from Paris, were written probably in the rude language of the times. But from the pen of genius, nothing truly

" Ep. Helois. 1".

can fall which may feem rude and uncultivated.
We have to lament, however, that thefe compofitions of Abeillard have all funk in the devouring
ftream of time : I have otherwife no doubt, but
the French nation would have them to boaft of,
as the elegant maiden-productions of their earlieft
mufe. — The Trouveres in the northern provinces,
and the more elegant Troubadours in the fouth,
had not then attuned their reeds to fing the loves
and the martial prowefs of peerlefs lords and
ladies. — The *roman de la rofe* is by fome critics
afcribed to Abeillard, but with no femblance of
truth : indeed, it is generally admitted, that it
was begun in the thirteenth century, and finifhed
by John de Meun, the gay poet of the court of
Philip le bel, a hundred years after [11].

Abeillard's fcholars viewed, with fentiments
of regret and pity, the falling off of their mafter.
It was an effect, however, for which they
could eafily account, becaufe, from his entrance
into the houfe of Fulbert, they had noticed its
progrefs. His fair pupil, they faid, was the
Dalila that had broken the ftrength of Samfon.
Fortunately, however, there was no de Champeaux to glory in his fall. — His connexion with
Heloifa could be no longer fecret : it became
the topic of general converfation. Fulbert alone

[11] Praef. Apologet. Bayle, letter A.

feemed

feemed ignorant of it; even when he was advifed
to look to his niece, he difregarded the admonition.
His love for her, and his opinion of Abeillard,
had tied a bandage over his eyes, which no
fuggeflions could unbind. — Thus, for fome
months, did the deception continue; and the
lovers were unmolefled in their literary amours.
Sometimes, that the old man might not be roufed by
the fmilleft fhadow of fufpicion, Abeillard affumed
the tone of a mafter, and even pretended to chaftife
Heloifa, as he had been empowered to do ".

The clap of thunder came at laft; the bandage
fell off; and poor Fulbert faw how miferably he
had been deceived. It was a fituation of deep
diftref. The man, in whofe breaft, he thought,
refided all the virtues, had betrayed him, and
Heloifa was corrupted ! His heart fank within
him. When he had a little recovered from the
fhock, his requeft was, that the feducer would leave
his houfe. Too much broken was his heart to
indulge itfelf in the ftrong emotions of anger
or revenge. Abeillard fays, that he only grieved ".
But he defcribes more fully, and with fome
affectation, the parting fcene betwixt himfelf and
Heloifa. How exceflive was their alllliction, he
fays; how much he blufhed; how his heart
was torn, when he faw the tears of the
dear girl; what a ftorm agitated her mind

" Hift. Calam.   " Ibid.

at the view of his fufferings; that they wailed
not their own mifery; it was for one another
only that they lamented. — Abeillard withdrew,
and Heloifa remained to meet the reproaches of
her uncle, and in folitude to reflect on the ftate
into which fhe was fallen.

But the reproaches of Fulbert fell heavieft on
himfelf: it was to his own wilful blindnefs he had
to charge the mifconduct of his niece. Abeillard's
treachery, indeed, was too foul a crime ever to
be forgiven, yet even here how glaring had been
his own folly! — Heloifa felt for the painful
fituation of her uncle, to whofe care fhe owed
fo much; but in the love fhe bore to Abeillard
was funk every other thought, which reflection
might have fuggefted. Confcience is filent, when
the ruling paffion, with fovereign control, holds
poffeffion of the heart. Her attachment to books,
reverence for Fulbert, ideas of religion, refpect
for the world, delicacy of female character, were
all abforbed in the admiration of the man, who
had feduced her.

She efcapes
with him into
Brittany. Fable informs us, that Argus, with a hundred
eyes, could not guard the nymph that was
committed to his charge. Love infpires a fortitude,
accompanied by a wilinefs of invention, which
no obftacle can withftand. Heloifa contrived to
acquaint her lover with all the particulars of her
fituation; and fhe acquainted him, with a
triumph of mind that expreffed the peculiarity of

her character, that she was pregnant, and must instantly have his advice in the courfe it might he proper for her to take; that her uncle's houfe was no longer a fit fituation for her ".

The necelfity of removing her was evident; but, confidering the fufpicious jealoufy with which she was guarded , the ftep would be attended with great hazard. Abeillard never found his invention on a feverer rack; but as he correfponded with Heloifa , who informed him of all that paffed, he had reafon to rely on her addrefs for fuccefs in the attempt. By a show of refignation to the will of Fulbert, his vigilance began to flacken: Heloifa therefore gave notice that foon she should he able to efcape. It was agreed between the lovers, that he should procure her a proper difguife, and that, the firft dark evening her uncle should be from home , she would be ready to attend him. They were to make for Britany, where he had friends who would receive her. — The day came. Fulbert, lulled into fecurity, had engaged to make a vifit into the country, and was not to return till late. Of this fortunate event, notice was inftantly given ".

The tedious hours paffed away, and night fell. Abeillard , with the difguife he had procured, which was a nun's habit ", was waiting at the appointed place: He received Heloifa into his arms; conveyed her out of Paris; and with all

" Hift. Cal. " Vie d'Abeil. p. 63. " Ep. Abeil. 5.

BOOK
II.

possible expedition , proceeded towards Britany, where his sister Dionysia, who had been apprized of the design , was ready to give them an asylum ". — Having thus disposed of his charge, the philosopher hastened back to Paris.

Fulbert , finding his niece had escaped, and suspecting what the cause was which had impelled her to it, was driven into the wildest rage. To his grief and first pain , was now added the sentiment of disgrace , which was brought on his family. But what to do , or how to revenge the insult, he was equally uncertain. When, in the paroxism of his fury, he thought of the most signal vengeance, and only looked to the dagger as his friend; the recollection of his dear Heloisa rose full before him, and averted the bloody purpose. She was in the hands of his enemies, who might retaliate perhaps the fatal stroke which should fall on Abeillard. — When , in cooler moments , he projected forcibly to seize the traitor, and to confine him in some place of security , he soon discovered how foolish the attempt would be: Abeillard, he heard, was surrounded by his creatures, was prepared against any attack, and was even ready himself to strike the first blow , should the smallest violence be intended against him ". — Again the old man had recourse to tears, and the unavailing suggestions of impotent passion.

ᵈ' Hist. Calam.   " Ibid.

Heloifa, in the mean time, was delivered of a fon, whom fhe called Aftrolabus. The motive for fo whimfical a name is not affigned ; but probably, as her own name was faid to bear fome reference to the fun, fhe thought proper to allude to the ftars in giving a name to her child.

The news of this event had a happy effect on the mind of Abeillard ; it foftened the high tone he had hitherto taken ; and he began to view, in a more proper light, the fufferings of Fulbert, and his own mifconduct towards him. " I felt, " indeed, for his fituation, fays he, and my " fhameful abufe of his confidence ftruck me on " the heart. " In thefe fentiments he waited on him ; he afked his forgivenefs; and he offered any reparation, which he would pleafe to call for. — The old man liftened, but his heart had been too much hardened by ill-ufage to relent fo foon. Abeillard proceeded : " And can you, indeed, be " furprifed at what has happened, when you " reflect on the charms of Heloifa? I am a man, " Sir ; and he that will caft his eyes over the " annals of mortality will find, that the greateft fages " of ancient times were made but the fport of " women. He only will not plead for me, who " knows not the power of love."— The eyes of Fulbert grew fuller. — " I will marry. Heloifa, " faid Abeillard, if that will give you fatisfaction; " but it muft be on condition, that you divulge " it not. My honor, my fituation in the world

H 3

" exact this from me." — The propofal was
unexpected, and a beam of joy feemed to fpread
over the old man's countenance. He was filent
for a moment; then he looked Abeillard in the
face, to fee if his words were painted there;
then he took hold of his hand; an action, which
at once faid that he forgave him, and that he
fhould have Heloifa ".

The friends, who were prefent, witneffed what
had paffed, and after mutual embraces, they
parted. — The whole tranfaction did honor to
Fulbert; but Abeillard clofes his narration with
a fhamelefs reflection: " He appeared, fays he,
" thus folemnly to fign a reconciliation, that he
" might undo me the more eafily. "

Serioufly refolved to execute his engagement,
Abeillard, without delay, fet off for Britany.
Heloifa was not apprized of his coming: but he
found her cheerfully occupied in the duties of
her new ftate. — I am come, faid he, (after
the firft falutations were over, and he had kiffed
his child, whom Heloifa, with the countenance
of an angel, prefented to him,) I am come to
take you back to Paris, and to marry you. —
Heloifa laughed, for fhe imagined, that he only
fpoke from gaiety, which was an ufual thing with
him. — I am ferious, continued he: I have feen
your uncle; he is reconciled to me, and I have
promifed to marry you. — If you be ferious,

" Hift. Calam. ,

replied Heloifa, it becomes me likewife to be fo; and I tell you ferioufly, that I can never confent to be your wife. — The firm tone, in which the laft words were fpoken, ftruck Abeillard with furprife. — Your affertion, faid he, is peremptory; but I muft hear your reafons. — You fhall, faid fhe; and then proceeded.

" " If you imagine this ftep will fo far fatisfy
" my uncle, as to appeafe his anger, Abeillard,
" you are deceived. I know him well, and he is
" implacable.—If to fave my honor be your objeċt;
" moft evidently you miftake the means. Is it by
" difgracing you that I muft be exalted? What
" reproaches fhould I merit from the world, from
" the church, from the fchools of philofophy, were I
" to draw from them their brighteft ftar : and fhall
" a woman dare to take to herfelf that man, whom
" nature meant to be the ornament and the bene-
" faċtor of the human race? No, Abeillard, I am
" not yet fo fhamelefs. — Then refleċt on the
" ftate of matrimony itfelf: with its littleneffes and
" its cares, how inconfiftent is it with the dignity
" of a wife man! St. Paul earneftly diffuades from it;
" fo do the faints; fo do the philofophers of ancient
" and modern times. Think on their admonitions,
" and imitate their example. — I will fuppofe you
" engaged in this honorable wedlock. What an en-
" viable affociation; the philofopher and chamber-
" maids, writing defks and cradles, books and diftaffs,

" Hift. Calam.   H 4

" pens and fpindles! Intent on fpeculation, when
" the truths of nature and religion are breaking on
" your eye ; will you bear the fudden cry of
" children, the lullaby of nurfes, or the turbulent
" buftling of diforderly fervants? I fpeak not of
" your delicacy which, at every turn, muft be
" difagreeably offended. In the houfes of the rich
" thefe inconveniences, I own, can be avoided:
" with you and me, Abeillard, it muft be
" otherwife. — In the ferious purfuits of wifdom,
" I am well aware, there is no time to lofe;
" worldly occupations are inconfiftent with the
" ftate. Is philofophy only to have your vacant
" hours? Believe me, as well totally withdraw
" from literature, as attempt to proceed in the
" midft of avocations. Science admits no partici-
" pation with the cares of life. View the fages of
" the heathen world , view the philofophizing
" fects among the Jews , and among us view the
" real monks of the prefent day. It was in retirement,
" in a total feclufion from noify folicitudes , that
" thefe men pretended to give ear to the infpiring
" voice of wifdom. — May I fpeak of fobriety
" and continence , Abeillard ? But it does not
" become me to inftruct you. I know, however,
" how the fages , of whom I fpeak, did live. —
" You moreover are a churchman , bound to
" feverer duties. Is it in wedlock you mean to
" practife them? Will you rife from my fide to fing
" the holy praifes of the Lord ?—The prerogative of

" the church may perhaps weigh lightly with you;
" fupport then the character of a philofopher : if
" you have no refpect for holy things, let common
" decency check the intemperance of your defigns.
" —Socrates, my Abeillard, was a married man;
" and the example of his life has been fet up as a
" beacon, to warn his followers from the fatal
" rock. The feats of Xantippe are upon faithful
" record. The hidden feelings of my foul fhall
" be open to you. Abeillard, it is in you only
" that all my wifhes centre. I look for no wealth,
" no alliances, no provifion. I have no pleafures
" to gratify; no will to ferve but your's. In the
" name of wife there may be fomething more holy,
" fomething more impofing : but I vow to heaven,
" fhould Auguftus, mafter of the world, offer me
" his hand in marriage, and fecure to me the
" uninterrupted control of the univerfe, I would
" deem it more honorable to be called the *miftrefs*
" of Abeillard, than the *wife* of Cæfar ""."

During this addrefs, Abeillard was filent; but
a conflict of paffions varying his countenance,
marked their ftrong emotions. Heloifa fixed her
eyes on his, and waited his reply. A paufe of fome
moments enfued. —My honor is pledged to your
uncle, faid he at laft, and it muft be done. —If
it muft, replied Heloifa with a figh that fpoke the
reluctance of her foul, it muft: "But God grant,
" that the confequences of this fatal ftep be not

" Ep. Helois. 1ª.

" as painful, as the joys, which preceded it, have
" been great "! "

Uttering thefe words, her eyes were raifed
towards heaven; and from the folemn tone, with
which they were delivered, it feemed, fays Abeillard,
as if her mind prefaged fome difaftrous event.

In this difcourfe, which I have abridged,
(indeed it is abridged in the original itfelf,) the
reader will difcover the ftrong fenfe of Heloifa,
together with her fenfibility and her peculiar turn
of character. Unprepared for the topic, fhe difcuffes it with infinite art, and is ready with
authorities, drawn from facred and profane
hiftory, to enforce her reafoning. — In the excefs
of her love for Abeillard muft be fought for an
excufe, if any can be found, to juftify fome ideas,
which, conformably with modern habits, will be
deemed licentious. His honor which fhe faw,
would fuffer, and his promotion in the church,
which matrimony would impede, preffed on her
mind with fo mighty a weight, that whatever
perfonal confiderations could throw into the
oppofite fcale, appeared to her eyes lighter, than
the lighteft feather. — Abeillard, as I have
elfewhere noticed, though a canon in the cathedral church of Paris, was not in holy orders, and
confequently was yet free to marry; but, by the
difcipline of the age, he muft then have furrendered his living, and with it all other profpects

** Hift. Calam.

of church-preferment. — " She complains that, in his account of this interview, he had omitted to record the greater part of the motives, by which she was " induced to prefer love to matrimony, " and liberty to chains. " She herself, however, fails not to supply the deficiency. The more she facrificed herself and her reputation, the stronger pretenfion she should have, she thought, to his regard; and in a voluntary attachment she faw a stronger tie of love, than the nuptial band. — The notions of the age were not, it is well known, fo fubfervient to legal rites, as ours are; indeed, they exifted not either fo numerous or fo obligatory; but I am far from pretending that, at any time perhaps, the romantic fpirit of Heloifa could have been confined to what, she efteemed, the vulgar rules of conduct. I hold her not up as an example to call imitation, but I view her as a phenomenon, which has my admiration and my wonder. The comet, which wildly roves through the regions of fpace, is an object of more eager contemplation, than inferior bodies which, tied in their fpheres, never fwerve from the fixed line of gravitation.

All things being fettled for their departure, and having committed the little boy to the care of his aunt Dionyfia, the lovers left Britany. Heloifa had felt the pang of feparation, in giving the laft kifs to her child; and her prophetic mind viewed,

" Ep. Hel. 1ª.

BOOK
II.

in every ſtep they took, a nearer approach to miſery. But ſhe knew when it was her duty to ſubmit; and having once fully expreſſed her ſentiments, ſhe would no more give pain to Abeillard by the continuance of a wayward oppoſition. — They arrived at Paris, as they had left it, in the ſilence of the night; for, that the prying eye of curioſity might not watch their actions, it was proper her return ſhould be kept as ſecret as poſſible. Heloiſa, with a heavy heart, went ſtraight to her uncle's houſe; he to his own apartments, and the next day, as uſual, appeared in the ſchools [a].

They are married.

In the courſe of a few days, the time was fixed for their marriage. Fulbert, whom experience had rendered ſuſpicious, was not willing to riſk any new adventures by unneceſſary delays. It was propoſed that the ceremony ſhould be performed privately, in a neighbouring church, before break of day. To this the old man aſſented. A few friends to each party were aſked to be preſent. The morning came, and the fatal knot was tied [b]. They then ſeparated, each one retiring to his reſpective home; nor did it ſeem, that the leaſt ſuſpicion had been raiſed. Abeillard made no change in his uſual form of life; he ſeldom viſited Heloiſa, and never but in ſome diſguiſe, or in the moſt ſecret manner.

[a] Hiſt. Calam.   [b] Ibid.

When the difgrace, which had befallen the canon's family, began publicly to be talked of; and it was known, or at leaſt, conjeĉtured, that a private marriage had taken place : officious friends ſoon interfered, who repreſented to the old man that, to retrieve the honor of his niece, and to ſave that of himſelf and his houſe, It was abſolutely neceſſary it ſhould be made public. Fulbert declared the promiſe he had made to Abeillard. Such a promiſe, ſaid they, is futile : to make ſome reparation for the injury he had done her and her family, he marries Heloiſa ; and this marriage muſt be kept ſecret ! — Fulbert was rouſed by the argument ; the recolleĉtion of paſt injuries ſtruck forcibly on his heart, and he told his friends, that their advice ſhould be followed. His ſervants received orders to divulge the marriage : he himſelf declared it in all companies ; and his friends were as induſtrious to propagate the tale [v].

The rapid flight of rumor has been celebrated by poets, and faĉts, to the experience almoſt of every man, have proved, that there is no exaggeration in their deſcriptions. The news of the marriage was, in an inſtant, carried into every houſe in Paris. Much was ſaid of the good fortune, which attended Heloiſa : while ſome ſpoke of her high deſerts, and others, with a malignant ſignificancy, hinted at the circumſtance which had

[v] Hiſt. Calam.

procured her the honor of the nuptial wreath ". —
The fate of the philofopher was not fo gently
treated: they lamented his lofs of honor, and the
furrender of dignities and preferment, which
muft neceffarily enfue. When the crofier and
glittering mitre courted his acceptance, he had
laid his hand on the diffaff, they obferved.

Heloifa appeared in public : fhe was noticed
with unufual curiofity; her friends crowded round
her to compliment her, ·on her new dignity;
and general gratulation founded in her ears. She
was thunderftruck, but not difconcerted. The
forebodings of her mind had told her to be
prepared for the event. With a compofed
countenance, therefore, fhe expreffed her utter
ignorance of what was meant; laughed at the
abfurd ftory, when it was more diftinctly repeated
to her; and when circumftances were urged to give
it additional force, with the moft folemn affeve-
rations fhe declared, that it was an impudent ·
falfhood ". — The reader who has confidered the
unexampled fenfibility, which Heloifa has mani-
fefted for the honor of her hufband, will not be
furprifed at this new trait of her difinterefted
magnanimity. In the fchool of morality a feverer
judgment will be paffed.

The firm but naif manner, in which Heloifa
denied her marriage, convinced many that Fulbert,
from views known to himfelf, had impofed a falfe

" Vie d'Abeil. p. 88.   " Hift. Cal.

report on the public. There could be no motive,
they thought, to induce his niece to deny a fact,
which if true, would bring honor and happinefs
with it. — Befides, when they reflected, how
brilliant was the profpect which lay open to
Abeillard, of rifing to the firft dignities in the
church, it did not feem probable, he would make
a facrifice of the whole to the charms of Heloifa.
When the beauties of Paris laid their garlands at
his feet, would he take up the chains of wedlock,
expofing himfelf to the ridicule of the world, and
to the anxious cares of life? — Abeillard, by his
behaviour, ftill convinced them more, that he
was not a married man. He had refumed, with
frefh ardor, his wonted courfe of ftudies; he
delivered his lectures with uncommon perfpicuity
and powers; he opened new and unexplored
queftions for further difcuffion; and his hearers,
as they were more than ever captivated by his
eloquence, rejoiced in the return of his former
vigor, and that philofophy had at laft triumphed
over the allurements of a woman ".

Fulbert, perceiving that his endeavours to
divulge the marriage, were fo artfully counteracted
by his niece, as to be almoft wholly fruftrated,
was extremely irritated. He charged her with
ingratitude, with infenfibility to her own honor
and to that of her family, and with a depravity
of humor, which, in fpite of the ftrongeft motives,

" Vie d'Abeil.

induced her to prefer falshood to truth. —
Heloifa juſtified her conduct with great firmneſs;
ſhe reminded her uncle of the ſolemn promiſe he
had made to Abeillard not to publiſh the marriage; and ſhe urged, with the moſt emphatic
eloquence, the reputation of her huſband, as a
motive which, in her mind, muſt outweigh every
other conſideration. " Accuſe me not, ſaid ſhe,
" of ingratitude: I feel all the duties which bind
" me to you; but Abeillard is my huſband." —
The argument was not of a nature to impreſs the
callous heart of age; the honor of family was
uppermoſt, and the wound he had received was
not yet healed [**].

Heloifa was ſilent: why remonſtrate with a
man, it was not poſſible to convince? But her
life became daily more irkſome. Fulbert perſiſted
to reproach her, and to reproaches added ill-uſage.
All this ſhe bore with a becoming reſolution: but
ſuſpecting this perſecution might at laſt end in
what ſhe dreaded moſt, the poſitive excluſion of
Abeillard from her company, ſhe acquainted him
of her ſituation, and of the fears which came
neareſt to her heart. Inſtantly he reſolved to remove
her from her uncle's houſe [**].

He conveys
her to Argen-
teuil.
Argenteuil, ſituated in the neighbourhood of
Paris, was then an abbey of Benedictine nuns.
Here Heloifa had been educated, and here ſhe
had imbibed all thoſe elements of learning; which,

[**] Hiſt. Calam.   [**] Ibid.   at

at this time, made her the firft literary charaĉer **в о о к** in the female world. Abeillard judged properly, **II.** that this would be the beft retirement for his wife: it would refcue her from the hands of Fulbert; it would afford her a pleafing fociety; and it might, poffibly, more than any thing contribute to filence the report of their marriage. — He informed the abbefs of his intention, and requeft-ed fhe would have a nun's habit in readinefs, as it was his wifh, that Heloifa fhould appear in the common drefs of the convent. Without difficulty his petition was granted: the holy fifterhood would be charmed, once more to fee within the walls of Argenteuil, the lovely penfioner, who had done fo much honor to their houfe: her engaging man-ners were yet warm on their recollection. — Abeillard therefore, again protected by the fhades of night, removed his dear treafure, and configned it fafely to the cloifter of Argenteuil [10].

Some weeks, it appears, had elapfed, before Fulbert could difcover how his niece had been difpofed of. Information, at laft, was brought him, where fhe was; that fhe had been conveyed away by Abeillard; and that, by his command, fhe had put on the habit of a nun. Appearances were ftrong, and on them the old man refted his conjectures. — Was a convent, thought he, the only place to which he could have taken his wife,

[10] Hift. Calam.

VOL. I.   I.

had he been determined to remove her? or if a convent pleafed him beſt, why was the dreſs alſo of a nun to be choſen? She might have remained there in the common habit of the world. — The ſuggeſtions of his friends ſerved to corroborate his ſuſpicions. They were unanimouſly of opinion that, Abeillard, finding it impoſſible to keep his marriage ſecret, had reſolved at once to rid himſelf of the incumbrance, and that his deſign was to devote to God what he could not retain, conſiſtently with his reputation and future proſpects. To attempt forcibly to drag Heloiſa from the cloiſter, would be, they knew, an act of ſacrilege; the laws, they knew, would give them no redreſs; other means of vengeance were therefore to be projected.

Abeillard, though conſcious of the uprightneſs of his deſigns, viewed, with pain, the maze of difficulties, in which he was involved: often did he wiſh that he had followed the advice of Heloiſa; but now it was too late. With a trembling eye he looked forward to futurity, but there no gleam was diſcoverable, which might ſeem to portend a fortunate iſſue to his troubles. — Sometimes he viſited Heloiſa at her convent, but always in the greateſt privacy [1]. — I will not pretend that he never indulged the thought that, tired perhaps by anxiety, to which there was no end, or from the love ſhe bore him, Heloiſa might propoſe, as the only way to end all troubles, to conſecrate herſelf

[1] Ep. Abeil. 3ª.

to religion. — He would never compel her to fo
fevere a choice; but fhould fhe herfelf firft fuggeft
it, it would not become him to oppofe her holy
purpofe. Liberty and independence would be again
in his poffeffion; and he might reach from fortune's wheel to the proudeft objects of his ambition.
The fight of his fair nun would, I know, difpel
this airy caftle; but when the gay hour was over,
and reflection returned, his imagination would
rebuild it perhaps in gaudier colors.

Fulbert, in the mean while, often met his
friends. His cheek was wan with anger, and a
fullen melancholy fat upon his brow. Various
fchemes of vengeance were propofed: fome they
rejected as impracticable, fome as too dangerous,
and others as inadequate to the infulting crime
of their enemy. It was at laft hinted, that there
was a punifhment, which would fully fatisfy
every defire that revenge itfelf could harbour;
which would carry pain and infamy along with it;
which would make the fufferer an object of general ridicule; and which would moft effectually check
his career towards further dignities and church-
preferments. The idea was inftantly adopted.

But even this project, when coolly confidered,
might be attended with fome danger, and with
many difficulties. Abeillard had innumerable
friends, and his houfe was ever under the guard
of fervants. The confpirators however were not of

a humor to be intimidated from their purpofe by any ordinary concurrence of obftacles. It was agreed that an attempt fhould be made to corrupt one of his fervants: this effected, what elfe could fruftrate their fcheme? The fervant, ·by a fum of money, was eafily feduced, and the plan of operation was determined ".

In the filence of the next night the confpirators affemble; they are five in number ; they proceed to the houfe of Abeillard ; the door is opened by the fervant; he conducts them to the apartment of his mafter; Abeillard is in a profound fleep; they feize the unfortunate man; all refiftance is vain — and the horrid deed is perpetrated ".

While the bufinefs, I have defcribed, engaged all the attention of the Parifians, nothing very interefting occurred in the affairs of Europe. To the tumultuary fcenes which clofed the century, had fucceeded a folemn paufe. It was an effect in the common order of things. The crufaders were returned; and the ftory of their adventures would fupply ample matter for general entertainment. They themfelves would be difpofed to reft from their labors, to enjoy the admiration of their fellow-citizens; and having expiated their former crimes, open a new career of extravagance and vice. But the calm, as the minds of men were then circumftanced, could not long continue.

Pafcal II.
pope of
Rome.
Pafcal the fecond was pope of Rome. He was

" Hift. Calam.   " Ibid.

a man of virtue and abilities, and Gregory the feventh had been his friend. The grand fcheme of ecclefiaftical monarchy, which Gregory and his immediate fucceffor Urban had formed, and begun to realize, was purfued by Pafcal. With their fchemes, he alfo engaged in their quarrels. Henry, the German emperor, whom the thunders of the vatican had not fubdued, was ftill living, nor was he difpofed to recede from his pretenfions. Again he was excommunicated, again the princes of Chriftendom were called upon to crush the proud enemy of the church, and his fon Henry was inftigated to lay his hand on his father's crown. The blow proved fatal. Unable to oppofe the powerful confederacy Henry refigned the empire to his fon: he was then thrown into prifon, but efcaping; he affembled a fmall army, which was defeated. The old man was reduced to extreme diftrefs; without a friend, he wandered from place to place, and fearing to perifh by hunger, he entreated the bifhop of Spire to grant him a lay-prebend in his church. " I have ftudied, faid " he, and have learned to fing, and therefore " may be of fome fervice to you." His requeft was denied. He did not long furvive this event. For fifty years his head had worn the diadem ".
. Though his fucceffor Henry the fifth owed his crown, in a great meafure, to the intrigues of

" Fleury, vol. xiv. Nat. Alex. &c. xli.

Rome; yet was he not for this more subservient to her mandates. He supported the same quarrel about the right of investitures, made Pascal prisoner, and extorted from him a concession of the great point, which had been so long in litigation. The pusillanimous conduct of the pontiff raised a general murmur: he called a council at Rome, to justify his proceedings, and to exculpate himself from the crime of heresy, with which his adversaries had charged him. But the council proceeded to censure what he had done, and they solemnly annulled the writing, whereby he had granted the right of investiture to Henry. Pascal confessed his fault; though what he had done, he said, was done by compulsion, to rescue himself and his people from the ruin which threatened them. He then submitted himself to the arbitration of the synod, offering to resign the tiara, which he was no longer worthy to wear. His demission was not accepted ".

An *investiture*, concerning which so much is said in the histories of these times, is a solemn act, by which the possession of lands and honors, belonging to episcopal sees, was conferred on the persons, who were canonically chosen to fill them. Temporal sovereigns pretended to the right of investiture. It was from them that the church derived her riches, and among her extensive possessions were many feudatory tenures, which

" Fleury, vol. xiv. Nat. Alex. sæc. xii.

naturally remained liable to the common conditions of fiefs. Thefe were called *regalia.* It was
afferted that, agreeably to general maxims, no
one fhould enter on the poffeffion of fuch lands
or honors, without the confent of the prince. —
.After due homage had been made, and an oath
of allegiance taken, he granted this poffeffion by
putting an inftrument, fuch as the paftoral ftaff,
or the fceptre, into the hand of the candidate.
In all this there feemed to be no infringement of
ecclefiaftical privileges, as it was not pretended
.that the prince could grant fpiritual or canonical
jurifdiction. This was left to the church. How-
.ever, as the crofier and ring, which the prince
ufed, on thefe occafions, were thought to fignify
ecclefiaftical power, it was maintained that the
ceremony was an ufurpation of facred things,
which belonged not to him ".—It muft, indeed,
be owned, that great abufes were the confequence
of thefe lay-inveftitures. Princes interfered in the
elections of bifhops, fo far as to deftroy their
freedom; they kept the fees vacant, under pre-
tence, that perfons were chofen, who were not
agreeable to them; they appointed their favorites,
men too often unworthy of the important charge,
to fill them, and fometimes, by a fimoniacal difpofal, they gave them to thofe who offered moft.
Againft this undue ftretch of power, the worthy
paftors of the church oppofed all their zeal; and

" Nat. Alex. ibid.   I 4

BOOK
II.

had this folely been the conteſt between them and princes, the approbation of all thinking chriſtians would have gone with the former.

Unfortunately both parties were jealous of each other, and this jealoufy blinded their judgments. They would not diſtinguiſh between things that, in themfelves, were totally diſparate. The temporal power apprehended, that it was the wiſh of the churchmen abfolutely to withdraw themfelves and their poffeffions from all earthly control: for which apprehenfion, clearly, there were too ſtrong grounds: while, on their fide, the church-rulers were not lefs fearful, that the prince aimed to arrogate the whole of their concerns to himfelf, to enflave their miniſters, to ufurp their poffeffions, and to control their elections. Nor was this dread lefs founded than the other.

In no part of Chriſtendom, was this contro-verfy agitated with greater heat, than in England. It was the difpute, which fo long divided Henry the firſt and his archbiſhop Anfelm. This worthy and learned prelate had adopted the new doctrines of the times, in which he was ſtrenuouſly fup-ported by Paſcal. Henry pretended to the ufe of no power that had not been exerciſed by all his predeceffor": but this power had been abufed. The court of Rome not fatisfied with attacking the abufe, aimed at the fubverfion of the principle. They would not allow that the inveſtiture of church-

" Nat. Alex. ibid.

honors fhould be given by a lay-hand whatever
declarations might be made, that nothing fpiritual
was intended.

When the characters of thefe three great men,
Henry, Pafcal, and Anfelm, are confidered, it
is matter of furprife that their differences could
ever be terminated. The inflexibility of Henry
was remarkable, and he had with him the general
fuffrages of his nobles and bifhops: befides, the
rights he fupported, were the ancient rights of
his crown. Pafcal and Anfelm were not made
of fofter materials, and it feemed to them, they
were defending the facred and unalienable privileges of God and his church. — On both
fides, I difcover the moft upright motives,
grounded on principles of equity and confcience.
— Pafcal at length gave way; though conceffions
were alfo made by the adverfe party. It was
agreed, that the king, in future, fhould grant
inveftitures, but without delivering the ring or
crofier; for on thefe implements, in fact, hinged
the grand difficulty. Pafcal, in a letter to the
archbifhop, thus expreffes himfelf. "It is true,
" I am difpofed to make conceffions to the king,
" that he may know the fincerity of my heart. If
" you fee your neighbour fallen to the ground,
" can it be faid you are in earneft to relieve him,
" unlefs while you ftretch out your hand, you
" alfo bend your body towards him? To give
" effectual affiftance we muft ftoop; nor is the

" attitude difgraceful ⁱ⁰." They are the fentiments
of a great mind.

Thus was the power of the church every day
growing to an immenfe magnitude : it was the foul
which gave animation to the political defigns of
Europe. — From this period we may trace its
progrefs, its alternate ebbs and flows, as circumftances directed. When it fell into the hands of
able and enterprifing men, no force was ftrong
enough to refift it; becaufe, on thefe occafions,
befides its own weight, it had the fupport of
thofe princes, whofe intereft it was to give it
efficacy. In the hands of weak or ignorant rulers,
its influence fell, in a fimilar proportion. —
Much evil, I am ready to allow, often proceeded
from this great ftretch of power; but alfo, very
often, did it produce great good. Could they
both be weighed in an equal balance, I fear not
to declare, that the good would often preponderate.
The popes, I know, were often men of ambition,
and in their defigns often not actuated by the true
principles of religion ; but alfo, far the greateft
part of them were confpicuous for their abilities
and high moral virtues : they were the firft men
of the age. In fuch hands place an unlimited
power, and the confequences muft prove favorable
to the general interefts of human kind. Every
motive, which has influence on man, was in
play to urge them to virtuous and laudable

ⁱ " Nat. Alex. ibid. Fleury, vol. xlv.

undertakings. Even their own honor was concerned: for a profligate pontiff was in no eftimation: and wherein could their ambition feel a greater indulgence , than in fchemes which tended to the fuppreffion of vice and the fpread of virtue? Here alfo fuccefs contributed to ftrengthen the power which produced it. In the twelfth century , take from Rome the vaft influence of the tiara , and the condition of Europe, I think , will appear to be greatly more deplorable than it was. It was the great engine which, in the ordinary courfe of providence, was deemed neceffary to conduct the bufinefs of the chriftian world. As circumftances altered, it ceafed to be fo, and it gradually dwindled down to what , at this day, it is. In fome future revolution of things, Rome may again rife to its former altitude, and be once more the controuling power of Europe.

In France, Philip the firft was dead , and his fon , Lewis the fixth , had fucceeded to the throne. Scenes of internal war and difcord ftill continued. Circumfcribed, indeed, as the royal domain then was, they were unavoidable. The proud vaffals , fome of them able to bring more men into the field , than their prince , little regarded his authority , when their tefty humor was irritated. But after the conqueft of England by a Norman prince, the French king was every day expofed to more ferious attacks. The Duke of Normandy was his vaffal, but alfo he was king of

England, and as such independent on him. Mutual jealousy and reasons of state could not long want subjects of contention; besides, the discontented men of both kingdoms were ever prepared to uncover the embers, and to blow the smallest spark into a flame ".

The vanity of an Englishman might be flattered in the possession of a territory, which led him almost to the gates of Paris; but when the evils are viewed, which, from this circumstance, so long desolated both countries, surely it must be deemed a happy event, that we no longer possess a single acre of land upon that hostile shore.

I mentioned the dispute about investitures, which was a very principal concern, at this time, in the affairs of England. What else engaged the monarch's attention was, the strengthening of his kingdom at home, and the establishment of his power in Normandy. As Robert, his elder brother, the hero who had done wonders before the walls of Jerusalem, was rightful heir to both countries, it required no small address to retain the possession of his usurped dominions. Robert, besides, was the courtier's, the soldier's, and the churchman's friend. But the good fortune of the English monarch prevailed; for Henry was the wisest man, as stout a warrior, and the greatest politician of the age, in which he lived. — The melancholy

" Hume, Daniel.

ſtory of the lives of Robert and his ſon William; **B O O K**
to which may be added that of Edgar Atheling, **II.**
the friend of Robert and his partner in affliction,
is well known to the Engliſh reader.

In looking round 'for other objects of ſelection,
I find little elſe in the political ſtate of Europe.
But the church is ever a fertile repoſitory: here
the hiſtorian, whatever be his character, philoſo-
phical or religious, can never want materials.

Enthuſiaſm, as the reader has already ſeen, was **Religious ar-**
a great feature in the character of the times; for **ders.**
mankind was then ignorant and unoccupied. In
this ſtate the mind falls back on itſelf, and finding
nothing there which may engage its attention, it
becomes always uneaſy, and ſometimes even
weary of exiſtence. External impreſſions are then
moſt forcible, becauſe the thoughts are unengaged;
and they are moſt pleaſing, becauſe they diſſipate
the torpid apathy, from which proceeds the
miſery juſt mentioned. But only ſtrong impreſſions
can generate this effect. Human nature, in a ſtate
of incultivation, knows nothing of the finer
feelings; the fibres, on the motion of which
theſe depend, have never learned to play. Thus,
in ſavage life, only war and the dangerous ſports
of the field are purſued with ardor. — The
obſervation applies to the twelfth century. The
trumpet ſounded to arms, and we ſaw whole
provinces at once in motion; at other times,

quarrels, invasions, skirmishes at home, could afford them an agreeable relaxation.

But as, in different men, different are the characters, owing to difference of organization, or climate, or education, so would not all be equally affected by the same agent. The voice or example of a man, deemed to be inspired from heaven; or the awful denunciations of God against sinners; or the horror itself, which certain minds, cast in a better mould, are apt to feel at the view of enormous crimes: these impressions, respectively, would produce their effects; and it appears that multitudes, at this time, were disposed to receive them. Whenever it happened, a proportionate enthusiasm would be raised on the mind; and this it was that, in a philosophical light at least, called so many into the cloisters, which were now opened in various parts of the Western world.

It is falsly imagined, that the monastic life was then a state of indolence or inaction, and consequently not calculated to generate the pleasing sensations, I described. In itself, abstractedly considered, it was not full of energy; but I have observed, that it often opened the paths to honor and preferment. Ambition would then be roused, and look ardently towards the object of its wishes; whilst the milder emotions, which religion and the exercise of the severer virtues, would excite in others, could not fail to produce the happiest effects. — The founders of thefe religious inflitutes, if we view them with a candid eye, will be found to have been men of exalted virtue: they feemed to be a new clafs of mortals, and to breathe from infpiration ; and it was thought, fometimes, perhaps, from an irritated imagination which blinded the judgment, or from ignorance of the powers of nature, or really becaufe heaven, in compaffion to a wicked generation, judged it expedient to fpeak to them in wonders; that they poffeffed the marvellous gift of working miracles. It may eafily be conjectured, how powerful would be the effect of fuch confiderations. Who would not wifh to be the difciples of thefe favored fons of heaven? By fome it would be expected that a portion, perhaps, of the fame fpirit would defcend upon them alfo, that they fhould be great, admired by men, and beloved of God; while others, more rationally difpofed, in a nearer approach to their perfons, would admire their virtues, and ftrive to imitate their example.

The monaftic or eremitical life was of very ancient date. It did not feem to men, endowed with warm imaginations, that our Saviour and his difciples had fufficiently departed from the common maxims and ways of fociety. So at leaft, in thefe degenerate days, we are fometimes difpofed to think of them. They fancied there were paths, which would lead them nearer to the high perfection of angels; and thefe paths they refolved to tread.

BOOK
II.
This it was that, in the firſt ages, filled the defarts of the Eaſt. No one would conteſt their habitations with them; and they earned their bread in the ſweat of their brows, accompanying their labors with continual prayer. The deſigns of ſuch men muſt have been meritorious, and in their lives there was perfection; but they muſt not be judged by any common rule. Man is a ſocial being, and there are duties, by which, in the ordinary courſe of providence, we ſeem to be bound, to one another. The fact appears almoſt incredible; but we are told that, at the end of the fourth century, the defarts alone of Egypt contained nearly eighty thouſand hermits ⁕⁕. The motives which led them thither were, I am ready to believe, founded on miſconceptions of duty; but the indulgence of paſſion could poſſibly have had no influence. When we ſeek gratification, it will hardly be among burning ſands and the howlings of wild beaſts.

This extraordinary love of ſolitude gradually ſpread from the Eaſt into the Weſtern continent. But as all paſſions partake, more or leſs, of the nature of the ſoil or climate, where they ariſe, or into which they are tranſplanted, the European conſtitution was found inadequate to the lofty flights of the Egyptian and Aſiatic hermits. — In 530 St. Bennet inſtituted his order in Italy, the primitive forms of which have no pretenſions to the auſtere

⁕⁕ Fleury, diſc. 8.

diſcipline

discipline , that distinguished the monks, I have
mentioned. In the lapse , however , of a few
centuries, even the disciples of Bennet fell from
the perfection of their institute. Such is the
nature of all human establishments : and towards
the beginning of the tenth century , by the
incurfions of barbarous nations and the general
hostilities of the times , which ruined monasteries
and overturned churches, the monastic rule was
nearly extinguished in the Western church ".

Now it was , that the famous institute of
Clugny, in France , rose from the ashes of the
Benedictin rule. A succession of abbots, famed
for sanctity and science , gave celebrity to the new
observance. Its houses multiplied over the continent
of Europe: men of the highest rank and of the
most brilliant talents , were proud to be seen in
the drefs of Clugny ; and it became the great
seminary , from which Rome drew its most
eminent pontiffs , and the church its worthiest·
ministers. But even the monks of Clugny were
men : riches flowed into their monasteries, and
the evils , consequent on riches, came along
with them. In two hundred years from its
foundation , Clugny sunk into obscurity. Peter
the venerable, who died in 1156, was the last
abbot, whom history records with praises.

" Fleury, disc. 8.

At this time alfo, St. Bruno inflituted his Carthufians. He was a man of letters, and of great repute in the churches of France. Difgufled of the world, and naturally of a gloomy difpofition, he affociated to himfelf a few companions, and with thefe retired to the dreadful folitudes in the neighbourhood of Grenoble. The man who has feen this fequeftered region, even in its more hofpitable ftate, may form fome conception of the mind of Bruno. The horrors of the place were congenial with his foul : here, he thought, the divinity loved to dwell, and that, in the howlings of the wildernefs, he fhould more diftinctly hear his voice. To the aufterities, with which nature clothed every object round him, he added whatever imagination could fuggeft, painful, macerating, and oppreffive, in filence, abftemiouf-nefs, and penury. The inhabitants of the Chartreufe, fo was their dwelling called, forbad themfelves the poor comforts of their own fociety; and the few wanderers, whom curiofity might lead to them, were refufed admiffion to their huts. Women were not allowed to put a foot upon the ground, which the pious folitaries called their enclofure; and Hugo, bifhop of Grenoble, to whom the wildernefs belonged, forbad the fifherman to approach their brooks, and the huntfman to difturb their filence with his horn : the animals of the foreft might not browfe on their herbage. Every cheering object was to be removed from this scene of prayer and penitence[*]. — Bruno died in 1101.

Though this imperfect sketch of the Carthusian institute may not seem inviting, yet so strong is the sympathy between certain minds and every thing which should seem horrible in nature and religion, that, in a short time, not only the Chartreuse was crowded with inhabitants, but even the order quickly branched out into all the kingdoms of Europe. The situations of their convents could not resemble the Grenoble wilderness, but the discipline and internal economy were every where alike. For seven hundred years has this order now continued, and what is extraordinary, it has departed less from its primitive austerity, than any other monastic institute in the christian church.

It is not the philosopher or the politician, who will be called upon to give his sanction to such extraordinary establishments; but to the infinite variety of character, which marks the human race, it seems, all possible modes of life should be permitted, whereby content and happiness can be procured. Man is a free agent, and may chuse for himself: there is tyranny in the contrary doctrine.

At this period, while Bruno and his disciples, in the horrid retirement of Dauphiné declared

[*] Fleury, vol. xiii.

war againſt themſelves and the allurements of the
world, Robert d'Arbriſſelles, in the milder climate
of Touraine, ſupported the ſame conflict, but in
circumſtances ſtill more extraordinary. He alſo
was a man of letters, and had rendered himſelf
ſerviceable in the church. He prayed much, faſted
much, watched much, and over his ſkin he wore
a coat of mail. His zeal againſt the faſhionable vices
of the age was flagrant, ſimony, ecclefiaſtical con-
cubinage, and every ſpecies of oppreſſion on the
poor and on the church. Robert had enemies; he
therefore quitted the world, and withdrew to
the woods.

Pope Urban being at Angers, the capital of
Anjou, in 1096, was told of the pious ſolitary,
and of his abilities: he wiſhed to hear him preach.
Robert attended, and acquitted himſelf ſo well
before a numerous aſſembly of people, that the
pontiff, on the ſpot, granted him an unlimited
commiſſion to preach, whereſoever fancy might
lead him. Arbriſſelles's fancy was not eaſily confined: he ranged into the neighbouring provinces;
multitudes crowded to hear him, and his ſucceſs
was wonderful. For ten years he led this unſet-
tled life.

Robert was, at laſt, made ſenſible, that great
abuſes were the conſequence of this promiſcuous
aſſemblage of men and women. Having no fixed
habitation, they wandered with their maſter, and
where night found them, there they repoſed.

Robert was of a more focial turn than the holy folitary of Grenoble: he held out his hand to the moft profligate finners, and women, of all defcriptions, were fure to find an afylum near him. His friends expoftulated very feverely with him; they charged him with too eafy a familiarity; they condemned his unfettled way of life; and they ridiculed his long beard, his naked feet, and his grotefque apparel. Robert looked round for an habitation, and he found one.

It was a wildernefs, called Fontevraud, on the confines of Poitou. Inhabited by wild beafts, and in that ftate of incultivation, which nature, in her luxuriant fancies, loves to form, it was of no value to its proprietors. They gave it to Robert; and here he fettled his numerous family. To protect themfelves from the inclemencies of the air, they built huts. Robert then feparated the men from the women. To the men he prefcribed hard labor, and, at ftated times, called them to fing pfalms or to pray: the women he confined to their cabins, and he turned the key upon them. For fome time, they lived in great indigence, fupported only by the wild roots of the wildernefs, and the water of the brook, or by the uncertain contributions of the neighbourhood. The profpect foon cleared: very confiderable donations in land were made to them; and the defart of Fontevraud began to fmile.

K 3

In 1116, ten years after its foundation, Fontevraud was in a flourishing state. Kings and the nobles of the land had heaped their riches round it. The number of religious of both sexes, exceeded three thousand.—It was a whimsical idea of their founder to subject the men to the women. He had read in the gospels, that John, the beloved disciple of his master, had been ordered by him to adopt the virgin Mary for his mother. This was an example to be followed: the holy women of Fontevraud were to have the privilege of mothers; and it should be the duty of their sons to serve them, and to obey them. Robert drawing near to his end, assembled the male part of his community, and said: " My children, is it your intention to perse-
" vere in the holy resolution you have made, and
" to obey the handmaids of our Lord, whom I
" have ordained to govern all the houses of my
" order?" They answered, unanimously, that such was their intention. He then chose for their superior, Petronilla de Craon, a noble widow, and soon after expired ".

" Fleury, vol. xiv. Nat. Alex. sec. xii.

END OF THE SECOND BOOK.

THE

HISTORY

OF THE LIVES OF

ABEILLARD and HELOISA.

BOOK III.

*Diſtreſs of Abeillard — Heloiſa hears the news —
Hard fate of Fulbert — Abeillard propoſes to
Heloiſa to quit the world — She is profeſſed a nun —
Abeillard becomes a monk at St. Denys — He re-
ſumes his lectures — Is cited before the council of
Soiſſons — Is confined at St. Medard — Returns to
St. Denys — Eſcapes in the night. — Reflections.*

Anno, 1119.

UNCHEERING was the ſun which roſe to

Abeillard. — His ſervants; wakened by the noiſe,
and the cries of their maſter, had run in to his
aſſiſtance, and procured him the help his melancholy ſituation called for. The neighbourhood
was alarmed; but the aſſaſſins had eſcaped. He
deſired to be left alone.

K 4

Now it was, that a thoufand diftreffing thoughts rufhed into his mind. — He that had been the idol of admiration, was become an object of fcorn and ridicule! — He fhould be pointed at in the ftreets; every tongue, and the eye of every beholder, would fay; there goes Abeillard! — How would his enemies exult in his fall; and even from his friends, he could only look for pity! Was pity at laft the enviable reward, that was to crown all his glory! — There was an end of literary fame; an end of philofophy; an end of every purfuit which was dear to his ambition. — Should he again dare to enter the fchools — but the jeering looks of the young men would be an eternal bar to the attempt. — Yet how much, thought he, had he merited this humiliation: and how equitable were the judgments of heaven! He had bafely betrayed the man, who had confided in him; and now treachery was returned for treachery '. — He paufed; but no thought would arife, from which to draw the fmalleft gleam of comfort: nor does he fay, in this tumultuary crowd of reflections, that his mind even once turned from itfelf to Heloifa.

The mournful foliloquy, however, was foon broken. Rumor had carried the tale from door to door; and it was hardly day, when his friends, anxious to know the truth, and to exprefs their condolence, crowded to his houfe. " The whole city, fays he,

' Hift. Ca'am.

" affembled round me: aftonifhment was marked
" on their countenances ; tears fell from their
" eyes. But can I exprefs, how much their lamen-
" tations irritated and difturbed me? The church-
" men chiefly, and more than thefe my fcholars,
" pained me with their fighs and wailings. It was
" their compaffion which afflicted me, and not
" the fmart of my wounds. I hung my head,
" and blufhed. I had read in the book of Num-
" bers, that fuch animals as myfelf were not to be
" received, even as victims, in the facrifices of
" the Lord '."

Vanity may be thought to have fuggefted the
firft part of this narration; but the ftory is told
in terms equally pompous by a contemporary
author '. In a letter of confolation to Abeillard, he
fays: " You were retired to reft, and meant evil
" to no man; when the hand of villany, armed
" with a murdering knife, prepared to fpill your
" blood. The venerable metropolitan of Paris
" bewailed the fatal ftroke ; the college of prebends
" and of illuftrious churchmen bewailed it; the
" city, deeming herfelf difgraced by the atrocious
" deed, joined in the doleful lamentation — So
" great, indeed, was the general grief, that you
" might be pleafed rather with the caufe which
" produced it. It is not in profperity that we
" know our friends. Paris, which lamented your

' Hift. Calam. ' Fulco, ep. ad Abeil.

"misfortune, has now told you, how much ſhe
"loves her Abeillard."

Heloiſa, in the mean while, was at Argenteuil.
In the ſociety of her dear nuns, in literary purſuits,
and in holy meditation, the hours flowed gently
on. Abeillard did not often viſit her; but left
freſh ſuſpicions ſhould be raiſed, ſhe had herſelf
adviſed the moſt circumſpect caution. When he
was with her, ſhe enjoyed his company without
danger of intruſion. Compared, therefore, with
what ſhe had ſuffered under her uncle's roof, the
cloiſter of Argenteuil had a thouſand pleaſures.
Imagination alſo helped to gild the ſcene : they
looked forward to the day, when, poſſibly, ſome
event, in the general revolution of things, might
be propitious, and make their union happy. —
Such was the ſituation of Heloiſa.

But Abeillard, for ſome days, had not appeared; the time he had promiſed to return was
paſſed; a vague rumor of ſomething diſaſtrous
began to ſpread; and it was whiſpered that Abeillard had been attacked by ruffians. Nothing is ſo
eaſily moved as the minds of lovers. Heloiſa
ſtarted at the ſound; the forebodings, which
troubled her, had not ſubſided: ſhe knew the
revengeful ſpirit of her uncle, and that he had
been grievouſly irritated; and ſhe knew the temper of the men, in whom he confided moſt. The
report gradually gained ſtrength; and Heloiſa ſoon

underflood the extent of her misfortune[*]. — It might, at firft, be indiftinctly conveyed, but the delicacy of the age would be no bar to the moft circumftantial detail of the tragical event. — Now it was neceffary fhe fhould exert her heroifm; fhould draw confolation from religion and philofophy; and fhould appear as great in affliction, as fhe had in love. — The felfifh Abeillard is again filent on the fubject, and no hiftory is extant to record the behaviour of Heloifa on this fad occafion.

The ruffians, I have faid, had efcaped; but diligent fearch was made by the magiftrates, and two of them were taken. One of thefe was the fervant, who had betrayed his mafter. The punifhment inflicted on them was agreeable to the notions of the age; they loft their eyes, and the *lex talionis*, (a law founded on the ftricteft principle of juftice, and which might, with the greateft propriety, be revived in all countries,) completed the work[†].

Nor were the bifhop and his clergy lefs active in profecuting Fulbert. He, as well as Abeillard, were members of the ecclefiaftical body, and confequently, the cognizance of their caufe appertained to them. Such was then the eftablifhed difcipline. — The unhappy Fulbert appeared before

[*] Vie d'Abeil. p. 96.   [†] Hift. Calam.

his judges : the crime, of which he was accused, seemed notorious; but, as he was not present at its perpetration, he was permitted to make his defence. What his defence was, is not related; only it is said, that he denied himself to be guilty. The circumstance of his absence, and the cruel provocation he had received, were maturely weighed ; the milder spirit of the ecclesiastical court was permitted to operate; and a sentence was pronounced, severe indeed, but not bloody as that which fell on his accomplices. He was deprived of his benefice, and his goods were confiscated [f].

We hear no more of this unhappy man, whose fate was peculiarly hard. Deceived by him, on whose integrity, he presumed , he might rely: and deserted by a niece, in whose happiness all his affections centered, is it surprising, he should fly to vengeance for redress? — Abeillard , with a selfish indignation, which a great soul could not have harboured, arraigned, as too indulgent, the sentence of Fulbert's judges, and called the bishop and his clergy , the accomplices of his guilt [g]. — Even Heloisa seemed to have no feeling left for the poor old man. In her letters she mentions his name with horror, and sees no alleviation to his guilt. When time and religion had worn off the edge of passion;

[f] Fulco, ut supra.   [g] Ibid.

possibly she would view his conduct with a more
indulgent eye: his name, at leaft, is regiftered in
the mortuary calendar of the Paraclet. There is
a time, it feems, when the moft refentful minds
forgive.

Abeillard was unable to withftand the humiliating
reflections, which preffed on his mind. The
philofophy, he had ftudied, was not of a nature
to fpeak comfort to him; of religion he knew little
more than its fplendid theory ; and his great
talents, the difplay of which had given exaltation
to his name, being once brought low, would
only ferve to add weight to his depreffion. His
friends in vain confoled him: their pity could but
hurt his pride; and their advice, he knew, was
unfupported by truth and the opinions of the
world. Like Prometheus, he felt the vulture at
his breaft. In this ftate of mind, he fays, it was,
that he looked to the cloifter, as the only place,
which, at once, could bury his fhame, and
hide him from the obfervation of mortals*. — He
communicated his defign to Heloifa, and propofed
that fhe fhould imitate his example.

Heloifa had not reached her twentieth year.
In the vigor of youth and the prime of beauty,
could it be fuppofed, that fhe alfo muft fee
charms in a cell, or that fhe would be inclined to
turn her back on a world, with which fhe had

* Hift. Calam.

hardly made acquaintance, and which, notwithstanding, had expreſſed a ſtrong partiality for her character, and an admiration of her talents. But the ſelfiſh eunuch knew the exceſs of her love for him, and of this he would avail himſelf: could ſhe be his companion no longer, the remainder of her days ſhould be devoted to ſolitude, and the pure colloquy of angels. — It is not ſaid, how Heloiſa received this ungenerous propoſal; but, as we know from her own letters, that the natural diſpoſitions of her mind were averſe from the cloiſter; it is probable ſhe would expoſtulate with Abeillard: ſhe would aſſure him of her unalterable regard; that it ſhould never be in the power of man to divide her heart; that the world ſhould ever-more be hateful to her; but that, as ſhe felt no inclination to the veil, ſhe hoped, ſhe might be permitted to ſpend her life, a voluntary recluſe, without the tie of eternal vows, within the walls of Argenteuil.

The proud man was irritated by this gentle expoſtulation, and he ordered her inſtantly to comply[*]. Heloiſa aſſented. " It was not religion, " ſays ſhe, which called me to the cloiſters: " I was then in the bloom of youth; but you " ordered, and I obeyed. " — The ſacrifice was not yet complete. She had, indeed, promiſed to comply with his injunctions; but was he ſure,

[*] Hiſt. Calam. Ep. Heloiſa. 1ª.

should he firſt engage himſelf, and leave her at liberty, that ſhe might not violate her promiſe, and return to the world He was therefore cruel enough to ſignify his ſuſpicions, and to inſiſt, that ſhe bound herſelf firſt. " When you had " reſolved to quit the world, ſhe ſays to him, " I followed you ; rather I ran before you. It " ſeems, you had the image of the patriarch's " wife before your eyes : You feared I might " look back; and therefore before you could ſurren- " der your own liberty, I was to be devoted. In " that one inſtance, I confeſs, your miſtruſt of " me tore my heart : Abeillard, I bluſhed for " you. Heaven knows, had I ſeen you haſtening " to perdition, at a ſingle word, I ſhould not " have heſitated to have followed, or to have " preceded you. My ſoul was no longer in my " own poſſeſſion " . "

Having ſubmitted alſo to this harſh demand, and chuſing the abbey of Argenteuil for her long reſidence, a day was fixed for the ſolemn ceremony of her profeſſion.

It was, by this time, no longer a ſecret, that Abeillard and Heloiſa had been married: the ſtory of their adventures was generally known ; it was known what had inſtigated Fulbert to his ſavage revenge; and it was now known, that the lovers were retiring from the world, and that the places of their abode were choſen.

²⁰ Ep. Hel. 1ª.

The day came. Curiofity had drawn crowds to Argenteuil. The bifhop of Paris officiated in the ceremony; and having bleſſed the holy veil, which was to cover the head of the victim, he laid it on the altar. The affembly ſtood in filent expectation: the gates of the cloiſter opened, and Heloifa came forward. — She was clothed in the becoming dreſs of the order; her attitude marked refignation to her fate; and the hand of afflliction had given to her features an angelic foftneſs. — As by a mechanical impulfe every boſom thrilled with compaffion: it had been whifpered that her facrifice was involuntary: numbers preſſed round her; and her approach to the altar was impeded "—They begged her not to proceed; they urged the fatality of the ſtep; they accufed her pretended friends of cruelty; they fpoke of her beauty, of her charms, of her talents, and of the horrors of a cloiſter. — Heloifa was vifibly affected; but not by their expoſtulations: the fate of Abeillard alone, who was foon to tread the fame mournful path, hung heavy on her heart: tears rolled down her cheeks; and, in broken accents, ſhe was heard to pronounce the words of Cornelia:

> O maxime conjux,
> O thalamis indigne meis, Hoc juris habebit
> In tantum fortuna capot! Cur impia nupfi,
> Si miferum factura fui? Nunc accipe pœnas,
> Sed quas fponte luam.   LUCAN. Phar. l. 8.

" Hiſt. Calam.

Uttering

Uttering the laſt words, as ſhe ſtrove to advance, the crowd ſeparated : her reſolution roſe fuller on her countenance: ſhe mounted the ſteps of the altar: put her hand on the veil, with which ſhe covered her face: and pronounced diſtinctly the fatal vows, which were to ſever her from the world and Abeillard for ever [11].

The heroiſm of this action has ſeldom, I believe, been equalled. But love and the peculiar ſtrength of her mind, would have carried Heloiſa even to more arduous ſacrifices, had they been preſented to her. — It will be ſaid, that her mind, at the awful moment of giving herſelf to God, was not in the diſpoſition of a chriſtian votary; that it more reſembled a pagan ſacrifice ; and that, inſtead of the pious ſentiments, agreeable to the occaſion, which her mouth ſhould have uttered, ſhe profanely repeated the lines, which Cornelia, with a dagger in her hand, addreſſed to the manes of Pompey, when ſhe received the news of his death. — It is true: nor did Heloiſa, either at the time of taking the veil, or afterwards in life, ever pretend that ſhe had any thing in view, than merely to obey the command of Abeillard. To have acted a part, inconſiſtent with this object, became not her character : She wiſhed not to introduce the affectation of religion, where nothing religious

[11] Hiſt. Calam.

was meant : the honefty and candor of her
mind revolted at the thought. Indeed, it is mani-
feft, had Abeillard but hinted that the action
would have pleafed him more, with a Roman
countenance, fhe would have met the point of a
dagger, or have fwallowed the deadly hemloc.

Years afterwards, turning to this event, fhe
fays to Abeillard: " I obeyed, Sir, the laft tittle
" of all your commands; and fo far was I unable
" to oppofe them, that, to comply with your
" wifhes, I could bear to facrifice myfelf. One
" thing remains, which is ftill greater, and will
" hardly be credited: my love for you had rifen
" to fuch a degree of phrenfy, that to pleafe you,
" it even deprived itfelf of what alone in the
" univerfe it valued (himfelf), and that for ever.
" No fooner did I receive your commands, than
" I quitted at once the drefs of the world, and
" with it all the reluctance of my nature. I meant
" that you fhould be the fole poffeffor of what-
" ever I had once a right to call my own. Heaven
" knows, in all my love, it was you, and you
" only, that I fought for — whilft together we
" enjoyed the pleafures, which love affords, the
" motives of my attachment were to others uncer-
" tain. The event has proved on what principle
" I ftarted. To obey you I facrificed all my plea-
" fures: I referved nothing, the hope only excepted,
" that fo I fhould become more perfectly your

" own. — For this facrifice, if I have no merit in
" your eyes, vain indeed is all my labor! From
" God I can look for no reward, for whofe fake,
" it is plain, I have as yet 'done nothing ".".—
" Through the whole courfe of my life, fhe fays in
" another letter, heaven knows, what have been
" my difpofitions. It was you, and not God,
" whom I feared moft to offend ; you, and not
" God, I was moft anxious to pleafe. My mind is
" ftill unaltered. It was no love of him, but folely
" your command which drew me to Argenteuil.
" How miferable then my condition, if, under-
" going fo much, I have no profpect of a reward
" hereafter! By appearances, you may have been
" deceived like others : you afcribed to the
" impreffions of religion, what fprang from another
" fource ".".

Ufed to contemplate in ourfelves and others,
human nature, as caft in common moulds, we
view its eccentricities with the mixed emotions of
aftonifhment and pleafure. Of this defcription was
Heloifa. She was born in a century, remarkable
for ignorance and a blind attachment to the weakeft
follies ; her education, within the walls of a
convent, had been little adapted to improve her
underftanding or to enlarge her heart; and, at the
time fhe began and finifhed the bold tragedy, I

" Ep. Helois. 1ª.   " Ep. 2ª.

have defcribed, the bloffom of life was but in its firft ftage of expanfion: yet already fhe was learned, to the admiration of France, and her mind had acquired·a boldnefs of conception, and a fufficiency in itfelf which carried her far beyond the ideas of her fex, and the adopted maxims of the age. In the moft brilliant days of Roman greatnefs, Heloifa would have been a fplendid character. — Her notions of moral and religious duty may be deemed too free: but my furprife rather is, from whence fhe could have drawn them. She had read, we know, the fcriptures, and fhe had meditated on the works of the fathers of the church: but, as in the fenfe and application of the doctrine, they contained, fhe was told to adhere to low comments and trifling interpretations, her mind was unfatisfied: fhe did not find in them that fublimity of thought and fulnefs of idea, which could meet the expanding energy of her foul. — She turned to the compofitions of the old philofophers; and fhe dwelt, with rapture, on the poets of Greece and Rome. Here fhe was free to range, unfhackled by rules, and ·unoppreffed by authority. In them the romantic caft of her foul found fomething which accorded with its feelings; and fhe became the difciple of Epicurus, of Seneca, and of Ovid, without perceiving that fhe had quitted the amiable purity of the chriftian fcheme, and the feverer morality of ecclefiaftical

difcipline. — When guides are ignorant, or when
maxims are fuggefled, unfounded on truth or
clogged with puerilities, a great mind is difgufted;
it begins to think for itfelf; and imperceptibly
adopts fingularities, perhaps extravagancies: but
they are the extravagancies of genius, and the
errors of bold nature. When the eagle rifes to
meet the fun, it leaves the earth and all its
beaten paths far below it.

Abeillard having completed one part of his
defign, haftened to the execution of the other.
He had chofen the abbey of St. Denys for his
retirement; and there he entered, a few days
only after Heloifa had made her vows at Argenteuil ".— The abbey of St. Denys fo celebrated in
French hiftory, for the munificent donations of the
living, and as the repofitory of the afhes of her
dead kings, was not then fo fplendidly magnificent,
as it had been. Dagobert, its founder, had
covered part of the roof with plates of filver; and
the internal decorations were anfwerable to it. It
is faid, that Clovis the fecond, at a time of public
diftrefs, unroofed the gorgeous monument, and,
with a more laudable liberality, diftributed it
piecemeal to the neceffitous. The Norman rava-
gers, in the ninth century, did not fpare this
fumptuous pile; they pillaged its riches, and

*Abeillard be-
comes a
monk at St.
Denys.*

" Ep. Helois. 1ª.

nearly reduced the whole fabric to a heap of ruins ". It belonged to the Benedictine order of monks; and as their revenues were immenfe, St. Denys foon recovered from its delapidation, and was in high fplendor, when Abeillard fubmitted his head to the cowl. But the monaftic difcipline of its inhabitants, which had been broken down, as it always happens, in the general defolation', had not recovered, in the fame proportion, as the edifices, which ftone and mortar eafily repaired.

A man of 'Abeillard's talents and reputation would be received with open arms. The joy was reciprocal; for here it was that he looked for repofe, and in conftrained lowlinefs of fpirit, dared to hope, that the world would forget him. The world did not co-operate with his wifhes. His abfence from Paris was foon felt; his fcholars (the number of whom, as a contemporary author relates ", collected from all parts of Europe, exceeded whatever had before been feen,) were vociferous in their complaints; they difturbed the peace of the city; and threatened to retire, if Abeillard could not be prevailed on to refume his lectures. Other profeffors in vain offered their inftructions. — It was refolved that deputies fhould wait on him in his cell ".

The philofopher had hardly recovered from

" Fleury, vol. xi.   " Fulco ad Abeil.   " Hift. Calam.

his wounds, and was beginning to tafte the gentle
comforts of retirement, when fuddenly his reveries were interrupted, and he was publicly called on to return to the fchools. In the depreffion of fpirits, with which he had juft quitted the world, confounded, penitent, and difgufted, the propofal, at firft, ftartled him: he. did not conceive it to be fincere, and he might fufpect it was rather meant to ridicule, than ferioufly to do him honor. He refufed to comply. On this they went in greater numbers; St. Denys thronged with the crowds: and firft they waited on the abbot, requefting he would permit Abeillard to come to them, and would even command him to leave his cell, fhould he perfevere in his refufal. They begged to fee their old mafter, and to him, in the warmeft terms, they urged their petition. — Would he, they faid, generous and difinterefted as he was, who had done fo much to gratify the world and his own defires, now do nothing on the more noble principle of ferving God and his religion? He fhould reflect, with what intereft, the talents, which heaven had fo liberally conferred, would be redemanded from him. Hitherto he had given his principal attention to the great and the opulent; it was time that the low and indigent alfo fhould receive benefit from his inftructions. — They hinted, with fome delicacy, at his late misfortune, and fuggefted that it had

been permitted, perhaps, for wife ends: he was now free from many incitements to vice, and withdrawn from the delusions of the world, that science might possess him more completely to herself. Now was the moment, they concluded, to become the true philosopher ". — These persuasions had not the desired effect.

But though Abeillard seemed so unwilling to re-engage in his former pursuits; it was not long before he was much disgusted with the manners of the monks of St. Denys. He describes them not only as men, departing from religious discipline, and addicted to the world, but as abandoned to the most shameful passions. The abbot he censures, in terms equally severe: " As " by office, he says, he was raised above others, " so was his life more criminal, and his infamy " more notorious "." — This account is thought to be unfair. He wrote it at a time of great irritation; when he had reason to conceive himself unjustly persecuted: to retaliate he dipt his pen in gall ".

Let there be some exaggeration in the story; it is still well known, as I have observed, that but little of the monastic spirit was left at St. Denys. — Abeillard naturally acrimonious, from circumstances rendered more severe, and mistaking, possibly, the effects of ill-temper for the suggestions of

" Hist. Calam. " Ibid. " Notæ Quercet.

pious zeal, hefitated not to declare his difappro-
bation of their conduct. Privately, and repeatedly,
he expoftulated with his brethren; but finding
fuch remonftrances ineffectual, he publicly arraigned the enormities of their lives, and, with his
powers of language, held up their crimes in full
view before them. — The monks were not
difpofed to admit this check to their amufements;
when Adam, their abbot, led the way to pleafure,
' was Abeillard, a monk of yefterday, whofe habit
had not yet loft its glofs, to become the cenfor
of his elders, and to replant the thorns which,
with the labor of years, they had been ftriving
to eradicate: he might purfue, with taftelefs
perfeverance, his own refearches, as he pleafed,
and they would not interrupt his lucubrations;
they only afked the fame liberty for themfelves,
which they allowed to him [11]. — What had fallen
to the lot of other reformers, Abeillard, I prefume,
was prepared to expect. His advice was difregarded; perhaps it helped to increafe the evil,
whilft he himfelf became the object of univerfal
diflike and hatred.

The young men from Paris ftill continued their
application, and the whole convent of St. Denys
was now difpofed to co-operate with the petition-
ers. The moment was favorable to both. Abbot

He refumes
his lectures.

[11] Hift. Ca'am.

Adam, fuch I have faid was his name, gravely advifed
Abeillard, as nothing lefs could give fatisfaction to
his fcholars, if he could poffibly furmount his
reluctance, to comply with their requeft; that
it was with much difficulty he had prevailed on
himfelf to give his approbation to the meafure;
that with pain he fhould fee him quit his roof;
but that no diftance of place fhould ever untie
the band which united him to St. Denys; and
that, on his fide, fuch a condefcenfion muft be
confidered as a heroic example of monaftic
virtue. — The holy brotherhood abetted the
folemn farce. — The flimfy fubterfuge was eafily
penetrated: but Abeillard, difgufted of a fituation
which difappointed his wifhes, and flattered into
better hopes by the perfeverant entreaties of his
friends, now thought proper to avail himfelf of
the occafion, and to accede to their propofals.
— Paris was judged too diffipated a refidence for
a religious man; and probably he himfelf, for
obvious reafons, objected to it: therefore a fmall
place in the country was chofen, where, in a
few days, he opened his fchool ".

The news was carried to Paris, and from thence
very foon it reached the more diftant provinces.
The conflux of fcholars was inceffant: there were
no habitations to receive them, nor could the
country fupply food for the multitude ". — Some

" Hift. Calam.   " Ibid.

authors fpeak of more than three thoufand, who,
at one time, attended his leffons ". — How
fcarce muft have been the means of inftruction;
or how ardent the thirft to acquire it, when the
reputation of one man could excite fuch a ferment
in Europe!

Abeillard now directed the force of his genius
to theological purfuits. He thought the ftudy
more analogous to the new character he had
affumed; but as his fcholars were very defirous
to be inftructed alfo in profane learning, to which
he had himfelf been moft habituated, he deemed
it proper not to neglect the latter. The charms
which, he knew, philofophy would take from
his tongue, he determined to convert to a nobler
purpofe. When his hearers, pleafed by the
delightful eloquence of their mafter, at once
admired his manner, and imbibed his doctrine,
he led them on from fubject to fubject, and
from profane to facred, till he could fix all
their attention on the great truths of revelation
or the fublime attributes of the deity ". — He
well judged that there is a gradation in truth,
and that the plaineft maxims or the profoundeft
difcoveries are but rays from one common centre.
— This method, Abeillard tells us, he took from
Origen, the firft of chriftian philofophers; and it
was moft undoubtedly excellent: but there was

" Vie d'Abeil. 129. " Hift. Calam.

befides a peculiar reafon, why Origen fhould be
the mafter he preferred to imitate.

It foon appeared, that the talents of Abeillard
were equally competent to every purfuit, and
that it was only exercife which had given him the
firft place in philofophy. He interpreted the holy
fcriptures, with the fame facility, as the commentaries of Ariftotle : and divine truths feemed to
owe as much to his expofition, as did the moft
abftrufe deductions of reafon. His fchool daily
fwelled with auditors, and the benches of other
profeffors were deferted. — If oppofition fhould
now be raifed againft him, it would evidently be
dictated by envy or low paffion. There was no
competitor or proud mafter to irritate

The fame of Abeillard extended, and the whole
college of profeffors took the alarm : fomething,
it was neceffary, fhould be done, to fave their
falling intereft. Two objections, it feemed, they
could raife againft him, and thefe they were
refolved to enforce. He was a monk, they faid,
and confequently the ftudy of profane literature
was obhorrent from his profeffion : befides, dared
he not to open the facred volumes of fcripture,
and to interpret their myfterious words, when
it was notorious he had never received any regular
documents from a mafter[16]? His treatment of the

[16] Ilift. Calam.

renowned Anfelm was well remembered. — On this ground the profeffors refted their oppofition; and they hoped to prevail. Archbifhops, bifhops, abbots, and the whole defcription of churchmen, were importuned to efpoufe their quarrel.

The method, which Abeillard had adopted, was highly approved by many; and they who, hitherto, felt themfelves oppreffed by authority, were relieved by the rational forms, he introduced into theological difcuffions. What he had written, on philofophical and literary fubjects, had been read with pleafure, and they flattered him that his genius, at leaft with equal facility, might penetrate the fecrets of religion[17]. They requefted that, to the authorities either of fcripture or fathers, which were generally adduced to prove the dogmas of chriftianity, he would fuperadd fuch elucidations, as might feem expedient to render them more agreeable to reafon. The introduction of obfcure terms, they thought, was futile; becaufe what they did not underftand they could not believe; and that it was ridiculous to fpeak of things, of which neither the mafter, nor his fcholars, had any fixed idea: fuch mafters might truly be called the blind leaders of the blind[18].

Thefe were bold notions for the twelfth century; but they were neceffary to difpel the Cimmerian

[17] Prolog. ad Theolog. ·   [18] Hift. Calam.

darknefs, which had fo long enveloped the chriftian world. When the feeds of moral or of phyfical evils have taken deep root, it is not a gentle effort which will draw them out. — The liberty of reafoning on myfterious matters had, by fome philofophers, been carried to undue lengths. Proud of their logical acutenefs, becaufe, agreeably to certain rules of art, they could form a fyllogifm, they faw nothing, in the whole range of grace or nature, which fhould outftretch their comprehenfion. Rofcelin, whom I have mentioned, had taken the lead among thefe philofophizing chriftians.

Abeillard, induced by the arguments of his fcholars, and not a little prompted by his own natural bias, undertook the arduous work. He would fhow, that the great points of religion were not adverfe to human reafon; he would render them more palpable by comparifons drawn from common nature; and from the notions even of the pagan philofophers themfelves, he would demonftrate how weak were the objections of modern reafoners againft the myfteries of revelation. With this view, he compofed and publifhed, in three books, his *Introductio ad Theologiam* [20].

Religion, obferves Abeillard, has not a nobler object, than the doctrine of the *Trinity*; and the names of the three perfons defcribe that being

[20] Op. Abeil. p. 973.

which is infinitely perfect. The name of the father announces power; the name of the son announces wisdom; and the name of the holy spirit announces goodness or charity. The union of these three constitutes perfection. — Nor does the distinction of persons rest here: it also tends to generate in the breast of man such sentiments, as may carry him to the adoration of his maker. On fear and love is founded respect: fear is produced by the ideas of power and wisdom: and we love that being, which is kind and beneficent.

It was this mystery, he says, which vain reason principally attacked; therefore he aims to defend it.

The founder of the christian system did but develope the mysterious Trinity. It was known, he thinks, to the prophets, and to the ancient schools of philosophers; and to the latter it was revealed, in recompence of their virtues. He praises the eminent qualifications of their minds, the purity of their manners, the excellence of their morality; and he dares to give them a seat of happiness in those regions, to which some christians, in too vain a partiality, pretend an exclusive right.

He then meets the arguments of his adversaries, and attempts to solve their subtle intricacies. He explains the nature of each person, and their differential properties. The language he here ufes is that of modern Trinitarians. — There exifls not in nature, he obferves, a being, in which a plurality of perfons fubfifls with unity of eſſence. It is only by analogies or diftant comparifons that any notion can be formed; and thefe muft be imperfect. — The co-eternity of the perfons he exemplifies by the light of the fun, which co-exifls with the fource of its generation or proceſſion.

From the Trinity he turns to the power of God, and difcuffes the high queſtion, whether God could have acted otherwife, than he has done, in the creation of things. He weighs, with a fteady hand, the principle and the order of the divine decrees. Wifdom and goodnefs, he fays, are the attributes, by which the almighty power is directed: they prefided over all his works. If therefore there be any good, which remains unrealized, it was his wifdom which forbad its eduction. Every thing has been made which power, wifdom, and goodnefs, could effect. More than what God has done, he concludes, he could not have done; nor could he have done it otherwife; nor was he free not to have done it. — This is the doctrine of Optimifm, which the great Leibnitz, in an after-age, more fully expounded, ftrengthening it with thofe powers of argument, which his vaft genius was able to fupply.

I have briefly ſtated the contents of this volume, which is written not inelegantly, and which
contains

contains matter of profound and intricate difcuffion. Abeillard boldly meets the argument; he
difplays a confiderable fhare of erudition and of
logical acutenefs; but if he flattered himfelf that
he rendered more intelligible what was before
obfcure, and has ever continued fo, his eye was
organized to fee light in darknefs. There was
novelty in his manner of treating religious queftions ; and that it was which pleafed his own
vanity, and raifed the admiration of his readers.
Lefs bigotted than his contemporaries, and lefs
awed by authority, the mind of Abeillard took
a wider range; but, at the fame time, he expreffes
a diffidence of himfelf, and a willingnefs to fubmit
his writings to the judgment of the church, and
to the criticifm of the learned.

The applaufe, which followed the publication
of this work, was great : it appeared that Abeillard
had drawn afide the veil, under which the doctrines of chriftianity had hitherto been covered;
he had done away the difficulties , in which
myfterious queftions were involved; and he had
anfwered the abftrufeft objections of their adverfaries [10]. Novelty of expreffion they miftook for
novelty of idea; unfounded opinions were to them
authentic documents; and in his weak allufions
to material objects they difcovered the ftrongeft

[10] Hift. Calam.

illuftrations of intellectual truths. — A work of
this nature was evidently open to finifter interpretations; and it could not be that his enemies
would view it with impartial eyes.

Albericus and Lotulphus, who have been
mentioned as the rivals of Abeillard, when he
ftudied divinity under Anfelm at Laon, now
came forward. The animofity, they had formerly
entertained againft him, had increafed with their
years, and had grown with the reputation of
Abeillard. Anfelm and William de Champeaux
were both dead[11]; and to their honors it was the
ambition of thefe two men to fucceed. They
were profeffors in Reims, and Abeillard feemed
only to obftruct the fpread of their reputation.
When the work, I have mentioned, appeared,
they read it; and it need not be faid, with what
difpofitions. Its excellencies were no objects to
them; but its blemifhes they conftrued into fhocking
deformities, and its cafual miftakes into monftrous
errors: his deviations from common language were
heretical innovations. He that looks for heterodoxy
will be fure to find it. — They waited on the archbifhop of their diocefe, and laid the impious work
at his feet[12].

For fome time had the good man been ill-dif-
pofed towards Abeillard. Unable to judge for
himfelf, he had relied on the affertions of others.

[11] Hift. Calam.   [12] Ibid.

Albericus and his colleague were loud in their accusations: their repeated suggestions alarmed the pious zeal of the prelate; and having raised in his mind a high opinion of their own orthodoxy, they now dared publicly to criminate Abeillard, and to demand the condemnation of his book. — By their advice, Rodolphus, such was the archbishop's name, engaged to call a synod of his suffragan bishops at Soiffons. The pope's legate was then in France: him they invited to preside at their meeting, that, with one accord, they might proceed to the weighty business. Abeillard was cited to appear before the council, and to bring along with him the work he had compofed. He obeyed[11].

In the mean time, his enemies were not idle. Albericus and Lotulphus had circulated many reports against him, and the minds of the multitude were inflamed to a degree of fury. He had dared to teach, they were told, that there were three Gods — Abeillard, with a few companions, confiding in his own integrity, and unfufpicious of the machinations of his enemies, went to Soiffons on the appointed day. His aftonifhment was great, when he heard the wild clamors of the citizens, and faw the preparations they had made to ftone him to death. They would avenge, they faid, the infulted honor of

He is cited before the council of Soiffons, and condemned.

[11] Hift. Calam.

M 2

BOOK III. their maker, and not wait the flow procefs of a council. Abeillard, however, efcaped, and prefented himfelf before the legate [14].

He held his book on the Trinity in his hand: " If I have written any thing," faid he in a fubmiffive but manly tone, "which varies from " the belief of my anceftors and the faith of the " church, behold me prepared to retract it; or to " make fatisfaction. This is the work, I have " written: take it, Sir; read it; and judge." — The legate, who is reprefented as a man of worth, well verfed in political intrigue, but as no adept in theological intricacies, very politely declined the propofal, and referred Abeillard to the archbifhop of Reims. The fcheme probably was preconceited: for by this means, his accufers, who were the confidential friends of the archbifhop, became his judges.

Albericus and Lotulphus, proud of the cenforial commiffion, with alacrity opened the detefted volume; they weighed its contents in the unfair balance of prejudice, and with wonderful malevolence, they mifconftrued, mifconceived, and mifreprefented. — If there be an eafy tafk, it is to defcry errors in the opinions of thofe who diffent from us; and never is the eye of criticifm fo penetrating, as when the zeal of overweening

[14] Hift. Calam.

orthodoxy animates the inquiry. Religion, which
fhould temper animofity, and give a gentle check
to the felfifh paffions , often ferves to imbitter
controverfy. We lofe fight of its high and
important character; our own feelings we ingraft
on the venerable flock; and we arrogantly fancy
it is the love of facred truth that infpires us,
when the bafe fuggeftions of our own minds are
the guides which point the way.

The holy inquifitors found ample matter for
reprehenfion : they were fcandalized by novelty
of expreffion; in words of an equivocal meaning
they could read a dangerous tendency to herefy;
and, at every page, their pious ears were offended; becaufe, at every page, Abeillard had
either departed from the old forms of language,
or he had dared to explain what they deemed
inexplicable, or he had attempted to make that
appear rational, the principal merit of which
confifted, they thought, in its oppofition to
common fenfe, and in a darkfome intricacy of
myftery. Still they were unfatisfied. A moment's
reflection told them, that the fathers of the
council might be more favorably inclined to
Abeillard than themfelves ; that his book really
contained nothing which was exprefsly heterodox;
that the learning and reputation of the author were
vaft ; and fhould he be permitted, in public
affembly, to make his defence or to explain his

BOOK
III.

own doctrine, it might be too hazardous to expose themselves to the impetuosity of his eloquence or to the danger of a defeat. They chose then what seemed the most prudent step: they waited on the legate; they magnified the importance, and the intricacy of the business; they talked of the multiplicity of their own engagements, which hourly called them off from the main inquiry; and they proposed, as other matters were to be debated in council, that the condemnation of Abeillard might be postponed to the close of the sessions. The legate assented [11].

Abeillard, during the celebration of the synod, was permitted to preach in public; and every day, from the pulpit, before a large concourse of people, he selected some point of christian belief, which he explained, agreeably to the principles he had advanced in his book. His discourses gave wonderful satisfaction: such perspicuity of language, and such a comprehension of religious truths, their ears had never witnessed. " Is this the man, said they, who believes in " three Gods, and whose doctrines, we were " told, are detestable! He now speaks publicly, " and where are his accusers to controvert his " assertions? The synod draws to a conclusion; " it was convened against Abeillard; but as yet

[11] Vie d'Abell. p. 157.

" we have not feen him at their bar. Have our
" prelates, perchance, difcovered that themfelves,
" rather than Abeillard, are in error "?" — Such
were the obfervations which all ranks of men
openly repeated in the ftreets of Soiffons. With
filent indignation his enemies heard them.

At length, the fatal difcovery was made by
Albericus. With inceffant labor he had wafted
the nightly lamp, and, in anguifh of mind, was
ready to defift from all further purfuit, when
a paffage, big with the moft noxious herefy, burft
on his aching fight. With exultation he clofed
the page, threw himfelf on his couch for a
momentary repofe, and was ready, early in the
morning, to wait on Abeillard. The propofition he
meant to bring before the council, clothed in its
moft horrid features; but how could he forego the
luxury of an anticipated triumph, over the
author himfelf, in a perfonal interview? He
was accompanied by fome of his fcholars. — When
the ufual complimentary fpeeches were made,
and they had talked on fome general topics:
" I have read your work," faid Albericus, in
a magifterial tone, and with a countenance,
which fpoke the fwell of his heart. — " Have
you?" obferved Abeillard drily. — " I have,"
continued he, "and in it my eye has fallen on a

¹⁰ Hift. Calam.

M 4

BOOK
III.

" propofition , from the horror of which , it
" will be long , before my mind recovers its
" wonted ferenity. " — Abeillard feemed rather
ftruck, and begged he would fpeak out. — " There
" is but one God, " faid Albericus. — " It is
very true, " replied Abeillard. — " This one
" God, continued Albericus, generated his word,
" which is alfo God." — " That alfo is true, "
faid Abeillard. — " It is true, obferved Albericus
" fmartly , and yet you dare affert, that God
" cannot generate himfelf! This is the blafphemous
" propofition. " — The laft words were uttered
with an air of the moft unbounded confidence.
— Abeillard fmiled: " I will prove the truth of
" that propofition , faid he , only liften to
" my arguments. " — What care I for your
" arguments , faid Albericus, your reafon, or
" your common fenfe: is religion to be weighed
" in their fcales? Authority, Sir, the impreffion
" of authority, is all I look for. " — " You fhall
" have authority, replied Abeillard : open that
" work of Auftin, which, I perceive, you have
" brought with you, and you will find it. "
Albericus turned over the leaves, but found
nothing. — " I will fhow you where it is," faid
Abeillard, taking the book into his own hands,
and immediately pointing to the following paffage:
" He who imagines that God has power to

" generate himſelf, is the more in error; becauſe
" not only God cannot do it, but becauſe there
" is no creature, corporal or ſpiritual, to which
" the capacity can belong. No being can give
" exiſtence to itſelf ". "

The young men, who came with Albericus,
were amazed, and bluſhed: their maſter was not
ſo eaſily diſconcerted. — " The paſſage, you
" have read me, ſaid he, after ſome pauſe,
" is eaſily ſuſceptible of a favorable interpretation."
" — It may, replied Abeillard; but as you
" aſked for bare authority, any comment, it
" ſhould ſeem, would be, at this time, rather
" unſeaſonable: and were you not, continued
" he ironically, ſo great an enemy to ratio-
" cination and common argument, I think, I
" could make it appear that Albericus himſelf,
" agreeably to his own principles, has fallen into
" the wild hereſy of thoſe, who maintain, that
" the father is the ſon of himſelf. " — At the
ſound of the word *hereſy*, Albericus was no longer
maſter of himſelf: what rage could dictate, he
threw out againſt Abeillard, reproaches, menaces,
abuſe. " The day is at hand, ſaid he, when
" neither reaſon nor authority ſhall avail your
" purpoſe ". " — He turned on his heel, and
departed.

" Aug. l. 1. de Trin.   " Hiſt. Calam.

The next day, which was the laſt of the council, before the chamber opened, the legate and archbiſhop held a long conference with the proſecutors of Abeillard, and many of their confidential friends. It was debated, what was moſt proper to be done with Abeillard and his book, for the condemnation of which the ſynod had been convoked. In the work itſelf, after mature examination, nothing had been diſcovered, which ſeemed to merit eccleſiaſtical cenſure, and the diſcourſes, he had publicly delivered, were univerſally applauded. The legate was diſpoſed to ſuſpend all further proſecution, and the aſſembly inclined to his opinion. A general ſilence prevailed; his enemies did but mutter indiſtinct accuſations; and even Albericus with-held the dreadful charge, he had threatened to produce againſt him. Gaufridus, biſhop of Chartres, a prelate venerable for his piety and conſummate learning, roſe from his ſeat, and ſpoke.

" You, who hear me, well know the profound
" erudition of this man: to whatever ſtudies he has
" turned his application, you know, what applauſe
" has ſurrounded him, and you have counted the
" number of his followers; the high fame of the
" profeſſors we eſteemed moſt, and that of his
" own maſters, you know, how eaſily he has
" eclipſed; and you know, that the wide branches

" of his reputation have reached from fea to fea.
" Should you pronounce a precipitate fentence
" againſt Abeillard, (of which I do not ſuſpeſt
" you capable,) what indignation will it not
" raiſe ? The tongues of thouſands will be ready
" to defend him. We have ſeen that the work,
" in queſlion, contains nothing which we can
" publicly criminate. Take care, therefore that
" you add not to his glory by any violent pro-
" ceedings, and detraſt from your own reputati-
" ons in the fame proportion. Would you wiſh
" to aſt, agreeably to the eſtabliſhed canons of
" diſcipline ? The way is open before you.
" Exhibit your charges in public aſſembly ;
" Abeillard ſhall be preſent, and ſhall hear
" each head of accuſation diſtinſtly urged againſt
" him. His own confeſſion, or conviſtion from
" authentic documents, will decide betwixt us;
" and the fentence, we ſhall pronounce, will
" impoſe an æternal ſilence on him, and meet
" the approbation of his warmeſt admirers ". "

This diſcourſe, diſtated by good ſenſe and a
juſt appreciation of things, was clamorouſly oppo-
ſed by the adverſe faſtion. " The advice is
" admirable! ſaid they: ſhall we enter the liſts
" with a man whoſe verboſity is eternal? Not the
" world combined could long withſtand his

" fophifms and captious argumentation. " —
Perceiving they were not to be prevailed on to
adopt the reafonable meafure, Geoffrey propofed
another fcheme, to which, he flattered himfelf,
the inveteracy of their prejudices might give way.
Having remarked, that the caufe was of confiderable moment, and that the council, from the
paucity of its members, was hardly adequate to
the decifion; he moved, that the abbot of St. Denys,
who was prefent, fhould reconduct Abeillard to
his convent, and that there, in a more numerous
and refpectable convocation, the bufinefs fhould
be maturely weighed and terminated. — To this
the legate and the reft of the company affented;
and the bifhop was commiffioned to inform
Abeillard, that he had permiffion to return to
St. Denys ".

Albericus and Lotulphus could not approve
this placid refolution: they faw there was an end
to their fcheme of humbling the pride of Abeillard, fhould his caufe be tried out of the diocefe
of Reims, where only their voice, they knew,
could command attention; befides, how humiliating was the reflection that, with all their high
words, they had done nothing, and that the
enemy might draw glory from their difgrace.
They waited on the archbifhop, whom they eafily.
perfuaded into their opinion: " Would it not

" Hift. Calam.

" reflect ignominy on himself and them, they said,
" that the heretic, who had been cited to their
" tribunal, should be allowed to retire, uncensu-
" red and free, as he came; and that another
" court only should be judged competent to the
" puny decision: who would now dare to check
" the progress of the insolent innovator, if the
" metropolitan of Reims must truckle before
" him"?"

Thus having obtained the consent of the archbishop to continue the prosecution, they directed
their attack on the legate. But it might be no
easy task to shake the resolution of a man who,
but a few minutes before, had, in a public
assembly, declared his sentiments. The professors
knew the ground they trod on, they knew the
character of the Italian prelate, and from the
experience they had just had of their own powers
of persuasion, they doubted little of the event.
Admitted to his presence, therefore, they repeated
the arguments, with many additional clauses,
which had so happily succeeded with the archbishop. The legate who, in the whole business,
had relied much on the opinions of others, was
not unwilling, in this instance also, to surrender
his own better judgment. "But, said he, if it be
" your wish and that of the metropolitan, that,

" Hist. Calam.

BOOK
III,

" the profecution continue, are you prepared to
" meet Abeillard, as this is the laft day of the
" council, and the bufinefs can be protracted no
" longer?"—The profeffors hefitated: the fcheme,
they had projected, they hardly knew how to
bring forward. "Does it feem neceffary to your
" Eminence, at length. faid they, in the gentle
" tone of adulation, that Abeillard appear in
" council; that he be permitted to reply to
" objections, and to make his own defence? —
" And can judgment be pronounced, without
" thefe conditions? obferved the legate with an
" air of indignation. —Abeillard, continued they,
" is a man, dangerous and feductive in his
" difcourfe: befides, has he not dared to open
" public fchools, legally unqualified to teach?
" And this bafe volume before us, did he not
" publifh it, and did he not difperfe it through
" the chriftian world, without the confent of his
" bifhop, without the approbation of the church,
" and without the fanction of the Roman pontif?"—
The courtly legate was vifibly ftruck by the laft
words. — "Why then, urged the profeffors impe-
" tuoufly, be awed by idle formalities? Let the
" book be condemned, without further inquifi-
" tion; and Abeillard, with his own hands, fhall
" give it to the flames. It will be an example

" ufeful to the daring infolence of future innova-
" tors. — The meafure is violent, replied the
" legate, but if the archbifhop and you, his
" counfellors, deem it expedient, I fhall not
" with-hold my confent, though I give it re-
" luctantly ","

The bifhop of Chartres was foon apprized of
the infamous refolution; and he waited on
Abeillard: he acquainted him of the whole intrigue,
and by what means it had been conducted.
Lamenting the violence of his enemies, and the
weak condefcenfion of the legate and the archbifhop; he entreated him to fubmit, with a manly
refignation, to the will of his fuperiors, however
unjuft or imperious it might feem. He remarked,
that fuch proceedings would bring infinite difgrace
to his profecutors, and that his own glory would
only rife more refplendent from the ftorm. He
hinted at what he had heard, that it was their
final determination to move, that he be imprifon-
ed in fome convent for life. He knew, he faid,
that the legate acted in oppofition to himfelf, and
that as foon as he fhould be free from the reftraints
of the fynod, he would immediately releafe him
from any confinement, to which he might be
fentenced. Other arguments he ufed to ftrengthen
and to confole him. — Abeillard was thunderftruck,

:" Hift. Calam.

BOOK   and the unexpected vengeance of his enemies
III.   unmanned him : he promifed to fubmit. The
bifhop again fpoke comfort to him, and, in retiring,
fhowed how much he pitied his cruel fate : his
good heart melted into tears, and they were
mingled with thofe of Abeillard[11].

In a few minutes, Abeillard was fummoned
before the council. He appeared. The legate
abruptly announced the final refolution. " It is
" our will, faid he, that you burn your own
" book."— A fire was lighted before him : Abeillard feized the volume, and threw it into the
flames.

The arbitrary meafure, and the promptitude,
with which Abeillard fubmitted, ftruck the
affembly. It was neceffary to weaken this impreffion : the legate, more than any other, fhowed
marks of diffatisfaction : a friend to the meafure
therefore whifpered in his ear : " I faw this
" horrible fentence in his book; that God the
" Father is alone almighty!" — The legate catched
the words, and rifing, with an amazed countenance, faid : " There is not a fchool-boy, that
" could err fo grofsly : the common faith of
" Chriftendom profeffes to believe, that there be
" three almighties."— *And yet there be not three*
almighties, but one almighty, jeeringly exclaimed
a learned doctor, who ftood in the affembly,

[11] Hift. Calam.   quoting

quoting the fymbol of Athanafius. — His remark was cenfured as a petulant attack, on the dignity of their prefident. — Terricus, fuch was the name of the hold divine, nothing daunted by the general clamor, proceeded in the words of Daniel: "Why are you thus foolifh, children of " Ifrael? Not judging, or knowing what is true, " you have condemned a fon of Ifrael; return " to judgment. You have chofen a judge, " continued he, who might inftruct us in truth, " and correct error; and this judge ftands condem- " ned in his own words: remember the fate " of Sufanna; and do you alfo free Abeillard " from the hands of his unjuft accufers." — The " attack was pointed and forcible; but fhould it " pafs unnoticed, the confequences might be ferious. The archbifhop, with much folemnity, rofe from his feat. "My Lord Cardinal, faid " he, in a fmall change of words, has fpoken " the language of Athanafius: *The Father is* " *almighty, the Son is almighty, and the Holy* " *Ghoft is almighty.* He who diffents from this is " a heretic: we fhall not liften to his defence."

He then told the affembly that, if agreeable to their wifhes, he would propofe that Abeillard make a public profeffion of his faith before them; that if orthodox, it might be approved; if heterodox, be cenfured. — The philofopher fhowed the utmoft willingnefs; but as he was beginning

VOL. I.

to speak, his adversaries called out, that his words
were not required; that the symbol of Athanasius
would be a better test of his belief. They
presented the symbol to him: " You may not
" be much versed in that sacred formulary, said
" they sneeringly, or your memory may deceive
" you. " — The ceremony, with all its circumstances, was too humiliating: the greatest man in
the literary world was reduced to the puerile task
of reading his profession of faith: any child, says
he, might have done as much. — He read, he
sighed, he sobbed, he wept; whilst his enemies
exulted, and the council, in secret triumph,
looked down on the fallen man [44].

·'As if guilty, and fully convicted of atrocious
errors, Abeillard was then delivered into the
hands of the abbot of St. Medard. This was a
celebrated convent in the town of Soissons; and
they meant he should there remain, as in the
secure confinement of a prison. The abbot took
him by the hand, and conducted him to his
cloister. — Thus ended the council of Soissons,
in the year 1191, much to the satisfaction of the
archbishop of Reims, and of those malignant
divines, who had so inveterately persecuted
Abeillard. At this time, he was in the forty-second
year of his age [45]. — The whole account of
this transaction is likewise, to all appearance, too

[44] Hist. Calam. ;   [45] Fleury, vol. xiv.

deeply colored, as I have already, on other occasions, remarked: but the memoirs of Abeillard are the only sources of information. '

The abbot of St. Medard was a man of great worth; and we are told that his monks were not less remarkable for their literary endowments, than for the exemplary conduct of their lives [16]. In such a society, Abeillard, it seems, might have been happy, if happiness could be found in involuntary confinement. They received him with the strongest indication of joy: but sympathizing, at the same time, with him in his hard treatment, they commiserated his fate; they endeavoured to console him; they censured the conduct of his judges; they applauded his heroic submission; they spoke of the number of his admirers; they reviewed the splendid career of his literary life; they extolled the erudition and wonderful perspicuity of his writings; and they promised him a greater increase of fame, from the lowering sky which, at the present moment, seemed to cloud his horizon. Could he be contented to honor their humble retreat with his presence, how brilliant would be the days of St. Medard! They, at least, knew how to value the treasure they possessed, and should it remain with them, their happiness was complete [17].

[16] Vie d'Abeil. p. 185.   [17] Hist. Calam.

The foul of Abeillard was .too gloomy to admit one ray of comfort: and the foothing fpeeches of his new brethren and their abbot hardly feemed to reach his ears. He begged to be' fhown to his cell. — Anguifh, fhame, defpair, there rufhed upon his mind: " And it is thus, thou " God of juftice, faid he, that thou fhoweft " the equity of thy judgments! Is it in chaftifing " the innocent, that thou pretendeft to vindicate " the ways of thy providence to man! If I am, " made to be miferable, collect all thy vengeance, " and crufh the worm, that merits not, it feems " the notice of its maker ".". — The blafphemous found fell upon his heart, and he paufed. — " But what was that misfortune, continued he in- " a lefs raging tone, which I once fuffered, and " for which I deemed myfelf the moft miferable " of mortals, when compared with this? Pain " of body bears no competition with. pain of " mind. I was then betrayed, infamoufly abufed: " but here my reputation fuffers; the glory of " my life is blafted for ever. My previous " conduct had then been bad; I own, it called " for chaftifement: But now, when the pureft " intention, when folicitude for the honor of " religion, guided all my views, and urged me " to the defence of truth; I am bafely traduced;

** Hift. Calam.

" I am treated as the enemy to God and his holy
" altars "." — His strength was exhausted, and
he sank spiritless to the earth.

The arbitrary proceedings of the council no
sooner got wind, than a very general clamor was
raised against them : indeed, the most partial
apologist could not pretend to justify such conduct.
The heads of the cabal were even ashamed of
themselves, and durst not meet the .public
reprehension. From their own, they tried to
throw the blame on other shoulders. The legate,
more than any other, felt the reproof of his
conscience, and freely censured his own weak
condescension: but to the intrigue and base jealousy
of the French faction, he said, the whole infamy
of the transaction was ascribable. The reparation,
he was able to make to Abeillard, and to the
violated rights of ecclesiastical discipline, he was
ready to perform. The bishop of Chartres could
but applaud the public displeasure, and if he
concealed the detail of circumstances which himself
had witnessed, it proved that the delicacy of his
mind kept pace with the honesty of his heart.
Even Albericus and Lotulphus were seen to blush.;
but versed in the quibbles of sophistry they could

** Ilist. Calam.

evade conviction, and almoſt ward off the point of cenſure [19].

Abeillard had been but a few days at St. Medard, when the legate, to ſilence the general murmur, and from a conviction of its expediency, and alſo thinking he had done enough for the gratification of a faction, whoſe abſolute diſpleaſure, it is ſaid, he was not willing to incur, gave notice to the priſoner, that he was at liberty to quit his confinement, and to return to St. Denys [20].

To quit confinement was a pleaſing circumſtance; but to return to St. Denys might not be quite ſo eligible. The news of the firſt, Abeillard received with rapture: it was an unexpected gleam that at once diſſipated the cloudy horrors of his mind; becauſe it told himſelf and the world, that his confinement had been unjuſt, that his treatment in the council had been unmerited, that his doctrine had been orthodox, that the flames, which conſumed his work, had been lighted up by the breath of envy, of malevolence, of falſe zeal, or of misjudging dulneſs.

To return to St. Denys was a ſerious reflection. His mind recollected the unpleaſant hours he had ſpent in that houſe of diſſipation; and when he compared with it the gentle manners, the religious deportment, the philoſophic gravity, and the endearing attention, of the monks of St.

[19] Hiſt. Calam. Vie d'Abeil.   [20] Ibid.

Medard, he felt a fecret propenfion which feemed to tie him to his cell. But the hand of arbitrary defpotifm had confined him there; and fhould he, from the freeft determination, refolve to remain, would it be afcribed to its real motive? No, fhould the confequences of his removal prove ever fo perfonally difagreeable, the world and his enemies fhould know that he was free.

His reception at St. Denys was not aufpicious. He read on the countenances of his brethren, that they were little pleafed by his return. For this he was prepared. He obferved in their behaviour the fame loofenefs, in their converfation the fame impudence, in their table the fame intemperance, and, at all times, the fame difrelifh for ferious application and abftracted retirement. Experience might have taught him prudence; but the natural impetuofity of his temper, now only exulcerated by ill-ufage, made him more fevere, and he repeated the harfh reproaches, which they had heard fo often from his mouth. — Abeillard refumed his ftudies, and in folitude fought for comforts, which the fociety of his brethren could not give him[18].

[18] Hift. Calam.

BOOK III.

Thus a few months paſſed. — Reading in his cell the works of Bede, his eye accidentally fell on a paſſage, where the venerable man, expounding the *Acts of the Apoſtles*, ſays, that Denys the Areopagite, whom St. Paul converted to the chriſtian faith, was afterwards made biſhop of Corinth, and not of Athens. If this be ſo, thought he, then are the monks of this convent, and the French nation itſelf, much deceived, who fancy they poſſeſs, within theſe walls, the body of the Areopagite; for their St. Denys, they inſiſt, was biſhop of Athens.— "Here, ſaid he jeſtingly, " to ſome of the monks who were paſſing by, I " can now overthrow your moſt favorite opinion:" and he ſhowed them the lines in Bede. — They read and reddened. "Bede, ſaid they in great " heat, is a lying ſcribbler: we well know " the thouſand fables, which ſwell his oſtentatious " volumes. It is to Hilduinus, abbot formerly " of this convent, that we give our faith. To " aſcertain, for ever, the important queſtion, " he travelled himſelf into Greece, ſearching " every corner of the land, and having found " the truth, he left it as a certain document " to future ages, that Denys, the Areopagite, " was biſhop of Athens, and that we, poſſeſs " his bones ".

" Hiſt. Calam.

It was no time for altercation; nor did the subject merit it. Abeillard only smiled, and was silent. But the businefs was not to be compofed fo eafily. They repeated their obfervations, extolled Hilduinus, and calumniated Bede. — " You shall tell us pofitively your own fentiment, " faid one of them with importunity; which is " the moft to be relied on, Bede or Hilduinus?" — Abeillard declined anfwering. They urged him to it. — " If I muft fpeak then, faid he, I own I " cannot avoid preferring the authority of Bede, " whofe works are read and admired, through " the whole Latin church."

The reply was blafphemous. Had he denied the prophets, or reviled the religion of Chrift, it would have founded lefs horribly in their ears. They called him heretic, an enemy to his country, and the calumniator of their holy order. It was now plain, they obferved, what had ever been his difpofitions towards the convent of St. Denys; nor was it lefs plain, how little he valued the glory of the Gallic name: dared he not impioufly to tear down the palladium, on which refted the fplendid fecurity of its fame; the holy patronage of Denys, the Areopagite, bifhop of Athens! — Abeillard in vain ftrove to footh their anger. He told them, he had himfelf formed no decided opinion; that he wifhed to be informed; that he had barely fpoken of the comparative authority

of Bede; that he entertained no ideas, hoftile to
the French name; but that, indeed, he could
not difcover, why it muſt be thought a matter of
fuch importance, that the bones, in their church,
ſhould be thofe of the Areopagite, provided it
were allowed, that their Denys was a glorious
faint[*].

The convent was inftantly in an uproar, and
the monks hurried to their abbot, to apprize him
of the event. He heard it with the mixed emotions of difmay and fatisfaction. It was melancholy,
he felt, that a monk of St. Denys ſhould dare to
harbour in his breaſt an opinion, fo derogatory
from its honor; but he was pleafed, that Abeillard ſhould be the man. Now, he flattered
himfelf, he ſhould have it more effectually in his
power to chaſtife him, than had had the fynod of
Soiſſons; and the reflections he had made on the
intemperance of his conduct had long hung, like
a poifoned arrow, in his heart[*].

The chapter aſſembled, and Abeillard appeared
before them. It was unneceſſary to expofe, in
many words, the atrocity of his crime. The abbot,
in folemn language, deplored his obduracy, and
threatened him with the heavy vengeance of his
own arm and of St. Denys. Nor was that all:
" I will write inftantly to the king, faid he; he

[*] Hift. Calam.   [*] Ibid.

" muſt avenge his own cauſe; for ſeditiouſly you
" have aſſailed the glory of his empire , and raiſed
" your hand againſt the ſacred diadem. Let him
" be guarded with the moſt careful vigilance , till
" my meſſenger return [*]."

Abeillard could hardly believe they were ſerious:
the whole buſineſs had rather the appearance of
a ſolemn farce: but when the countenance of his
abbot, and the geſtures of the monks, had convinced him they were in earneſt: " If I have been
" guilty of any fault , ſaid he , I am ready to
" ſubmit to whatever puniſhment, in the order
" of monaſtic diſcipline, you may judge proper
" to inflict."— He was not heard , and they dragged
him to his cell.

The reader, who may know, with what warmth,
this queſtion, even in the moſt enlightened period,
has been agitated by the French critics, will not
be ſurpriſed that, in the twelfth century, in the
convent itſelf of St. Denys, it ſhould have raiſed
ſuch a ferment. At length, I believe , the weighty
point is decided; for it ſeems generally agreed
among the learned, that Denys the Areopagite
ſuffered martyrdom at Athens in the year 95 ; and
that the other Denys did not come into France
till towards the beginning of the third century.
He was made firſt biſhop of Paris , and was

[*] Hiſt. Calam.

martyred fome years after; when as abbot Hilduinus, the author of the whole fable, whom I have
mentioned, relates, he picked up his own head
from the ground, and walked away with it. His
body refls in the noble abbey which bears his
name ".

*He efcapes
in the night.* Abeillard, though again in defolation, was not
difpofed to fink under it. This new infult was
exafperating, and it roufed his paffions. If
fortune had confpired againft him, and the world
muft be his foe, he had himfelf only to look to:
and where is the man who bears not within his
own breaft an anchor, on which he may fecurely
reft, when billows roll around him? But it was
not prudent to expofe himfelf to all the fury of
his enemies, nor to wait till the meffenger fhould
return from the king. The exaggerated and falfe
reports, which would be carried to his majefty,
might roufe him to too fignal a vengeance. He
determined to efcape from St. Denys.

This efcape, however, could not be fo eafily
effected. The guards that watched him were
vigilant, and they were animated to their office
by the fevere orders of their fuperiors, and by
their own perfonal diflike to the prifoner. But
for the honor of human nature, never was there
a man in diftrefs, who did not find a friend.—

" Fleury, Nat. Alex. and others.

Among the monks of St. Denys were some few, who could see the exalted virtues of Abeillard, and could admire them; who could behold the depraved conduct of their brethren, and could pity Abeillard who was expofed to their refentment. Abeillard in their looks read the emotions of their hearts: they had eluded his keepers, and approached him, and he faw the tear of compaffion ftanding in their eyes. He opened his heart to them, and told them his defign. — " We will " favor your efcape, faid they; fear not. We " are men, and pity you. When the convent " fhall be funk to reft, be ready at the door of " your cell: leave the reft to us."— The hour came: fome of his old fcholars, who had engaged to be the companions of his flight, were pofted near the convent: his keepers were bribed or withdrawn: the fignal was given; and Abeillard came out from his cell, bleffing the indulgent night, which, more than once, had been propitious to his defigns [11].

When we review thefe extraordinary fcenes, in which Abeillard has been engaged, we fhall certainly be difpofed to think rather favorably of him. In the firft part of his life, a natural petulance of mind, heightened by ambition, and often by vanity, had hurried him into controverfy, and acrid altercations with his mafters. When he

[11] Hift. Calam. Vie d'Abeil. p. 206.

fuffered, we did not pity him. — The tragical event,
which then fucceeded, we alfo afcribed to his
own mifconduct; and I think, we may fay, that
he deferved it. — But we have lately beheld him
perfecuted without caufe, fmarting under the lafh
of malevolence, traduced where praife fhould have
crowned his labors, and made a butt, againft
which, ignorance and falfe zeal, dulnefs and
rancorous jealoufy, pride and licentious depravity,
directed their fhafts. — The exultation of mind
which fwelled his heart in profperity, feemed
to leave him fo enfeebled, when the hour of
diftrefs came, that, like a reed, the gentleft blaft
could bend him. He poffeffed not the ordinary
courage of a man: he defponded, hung his head,
and looked for the womanly confolation of folacing
his grief in tears.

These obfervations muft be juft; for they are
founded on the very circumftantial detail he gives
of his own adventures and fufferings. When he
fpeaks of his own weakneffes, he may be credited:
he even feems to have indulged an extraordinary
vanity in the narration: but in the account he
gives of other men, of their tranfactions, and of
the motives by which, he fays, they were led,
great allowance muft be made; and I am fometimes almoft inclined to believe, that he loved
himfelf, better than he did truth: or, at all
events, fo dark was the medium, through which
he viewed the conduct of others, as it related to

himfelf, that he had it not in his power to form an equitable and candid judgment. Round his own perfon played a bright and brilliant funfhine, which caft light and amiability on every thought, every defign, every undertaking, every action. So he fancied. — Such was Abeillard.

Heloifa he feemed to have forgotten. Abforbed in himfelf, where was the object, that deferved a moment's thought, if it could not minifter to his own happinefs? The fancied magnitude of his misfortunes fo filled his mind, that there was no room for the cares of others. Heloifa, immured in her cell, could give joy to no other man, and Abeillard was fatisfied. Alluding to this period, fhe fays to him: " But 'how has it happened, tell " me, that after my retreat from the world, " which was all your own work, I have been fo " neglected, or fo forgotten, that you never came, " either perfonally to recreate my folitude, or " ever wrote a line to confole me. If you can, " account for this conduct; or I muft tell you my own " fufpicions, which are alfo the general fufpicions " of the world. It was paffion, Abeillard, and " not friendfhip, which drew you to me; it was " not love, but a more bafe propenfion. The " incitements to pleafure removed, every other " more honorable fentiment, to which they might " feem to give life, has vanifhed with them "."

'' Ep. Heloif. 1ª.

The perfecutions, to which his doctrinal ideas
expofed him, give a ftrong portrait, of the times;
but it is a portrait, I fear, which, with fome little
variation, may be made to reprefent almoft every
era of human exiftence. Yet we are ftruck when
we fee Abeillard before the council of Soiffons,
treated with fuch unmerited feverity, and we feel
comfort in the reflection, that we do not live in
fo intolerant an age. Comfort we may feel; but
he, I think, who, with fome attention, has
obferved the real character even of the prefent
times, will be ready to aknowledge that, if they
are lefs intolerant, it is not becaufe either their
principles or their paffions are different, but
becaufe they dare not, or are afhamed, to
profefs them. The philofophy of a few, the
chriftian moderation of others, the religious
indifference of many, and the modifh vices of
more, have gained fo much on the bigotry, the
fuperftition, the falfe zeal, the fanaticifm of the
multitude, that he who dares to be intolerant is
laughed at, and he who would perfecute is
ridiculed.

Yet what are the points which, in the times I
am defcribing, could fo warm the breafts of
churchmen, and which, in 1786, would perhaps
communicate to the fame order of men an equal
portion of holy fire, were the impediments
removed, which I have mentioned? View
them

them abstractedly, as they are generally considered, and it will be found that, they regard not the important worship of our maker, nor the great interests of religion, nor the good of society, nor moral worth, nor our own improvement in virtue, justice, and piety. It has been said, with some semblance of truth, that the holy founder of the christian system, therefore expressed certain doctrines in ambiguous or mysterious language, that men who, he knew, from variety of character, could never adopt unity in belief, might not indeed be free to think as they pleased, (for his language is sufficiently perspicuous,) but that, when they differed from one another, they might find indulgence. If such was his intention, how much have we striven to counteract the wise arrangement? We have quarrelled, and have persecuted, and have tormented one another, with as much presumption, and with the same stubborn acrimony, even when we owned the matters in litigation were impenetrable to human reason, as if they had been self-evident principles, or the most obvious maxims in common life.

And what is it that can rouse this preternatural zeal? When our interest is engaged, or the business comes home to our own feelings, then, I conceive, we may be ardent, we may rush into opposition, or into faction: but when the object is as remote as earth from heaven; when it constitutes,

BOOK
III.

perhaps, a part of thofe effential attributes, which the deity has pleafed to conceal from us, in the dark abyfs of his own infinitude: when he has not conflituted us his delegates, to reprefent his perfon, or to vindicate his rights: why are we arrogantly to erect a tribunal, and call our equals before it? He who made us what we are, would very willingly, I prefume, difpenfe with the forwardnefs of our zeal, and be more fatisfied, that we lived as men, in the improvement of our own natures, and left the things above us to that adminiftration, the wifdom and beneficence of which are beft adapted to the important work.

END OF THE THIRD BOOK.

THE
HISTORY
OF THE LIVES OF
ABEILLARD and HELOISA.

BOOK IV.

*The count of Champagne protects Abeillard — The
story of Stephen de Garlande — Abeillard retires
into the forest of Nogent — He is visited in the
forest, and again begins to teach — He builds the
Paraclet — Norbert of Premontré — Bernard of
Clairvaux — Miracles — Abeillard is chosen abbot
of St. Gildas — Argenteuil taken from the nuns —
Heloisa goes to Paraclet — Abeillard is again cenfured — He fixes at St. Gildas, and is perfecuted by
his monks.*

Anno, 1122.

ABEILLARD, with the few companions of
his flight, found himself, by break of day, not
far from the fpot, to which he had retired, and
where he had taught, when, as the reader will
recollect, he was fuddenly called before the fynod
of Soiffons. The place, indeed, belonged to the

BOOK
VI.

The count of
Champagne
protects
Abeillard.

abbey of St. Denys, but it lay in the territories of the count of Champagne[^1]. The count, named Theobald, though a vaſſal of the French king, was, in other regards, agreeably to the feudatory tenures of the age, an independent prince. Here, ſhould the abbot of St. Denys be diſpoſed to proſecute his ſubject; or. ſhould Lewis of France attempt to puniſh the culprit, who had dared to think that the patron of his nation might not have been biſhop of Athens, Abeillard knew he ſhould be ſecure, and be protected from inſult.

Theobald, a nobleman of ſplendid virtues, and the great patron of learning, was no ſtranger to the character of Abeillard. He had ſeen him, on former occaſions, and he had heard the ſtory of his misfortunes and his oppreſſions: he received him with proper marks of attention; and having inquired into the cauſe of a viſit ſo unexpected; " In what, ſaid he, can I ſerve " you, Abeillard?"—The philoſopher only aſked for an aſylum, for the common protection which the perſecuted may claim.

Near to the gates of Provins, a ſmall town in Champagne, was ſituated a monaſtery, the prior of which was the intimate friend of Abeillard. To the roof of this friend he begged leave to retire; and the favor was inſtantly granted. The

' Hiſt. Calam.

good prior came out to meet him; and his countenance shewed that warmth of benevolence, which
the full heart, on such occasions only, can express.
Abeillard entered, and felt himself happy: he
had escaped from danger, and he was now in the
arms of a sincere and sympathizing friend[*].

In the collection of his works is a letter, which
he seems to have written, immediately on his
arrival at Provins, to the abbot and monks of
St. Denys. It is addressed, in the language of
insincerity, to *his most dear father, Adam, by the
grace of God, abbot of St. Denys, and to his beloved
brothers and co-monks.* Himself he styles, *a monk in
dress, in conduct a sinner.* — He says not a word of
his precipitate flight, nor alludes to any circumstance of his present situation. The whole letter
is on the ridiculous dispute about Denys, the
Areopagite. Having considered the point more
maturely, or apprehensive, perhaps, that the
enemy might dare to pursue him into his secure
intrenchments, he is disposed to give up the
authority of Bede, and to join those, whose
weight, he thinks, should preponderate. It is a
weak piece of criticism, and does no more honor
to his head, than it did to his heart. What effect
it had at St. Denys, we are not told: Abeillard,
in his memoirs, does not even mention the
circumstance of having written the letter.

[*] Hist. Calam.

He had not been many days at St. Ayoul, such
was the name of the convent, when, to his great
furprife, he was informed, that the abbot of
St. Denys was come to Provins. It was a vifit to
the count, on bufinefs regarding his monaflery.
Abeillard thought the moment favorable; and
fhould he be able to prevail on the count, to be
his interceffor, he doubted little of the fuccefs of
his fcheme. In company of the prior he waited
on Theobald: his requeft was, that he would
petition the abbot to pardon the fault he had
committed, by leaving his cell without permiffion,
and that he would grant him leave to practife the
life of a monk, in any retirement, which might
be agreeable to him[1].

The abbot heard the propofal with attention;
and he anfwered the count, that he was forry it
was not in his power immediately to comply
with his requeft, but that he would lay it before
the monks, who had accompanied him, and that,
before night, the refult of their opinions fhould
be notified to him. —The confraternity affembled.
It was very evident, they thought, that Abeillard's
intention was to retire into fome other convent;
and would not this reflect difhonor on St. Denys?
However much his conduct might be difpleafing
to them; he was a man of vaft erudition, raifed

[1] H. ft. Calam.

to the higheft pitch of literary glory; was admired by the world, and muft be confidered as a jewel of immenfe value, which they could not furrender into other hands. When he had taken the refolution of quitting the world, it was St. Denys he had preferred to every other monaftic eftablifhment. — They therefore unanimoufly refolved not to comply with his requifition; and the fame was made known to the count of Champagne. They went further: on the fpot, it was fignified to Abeillard that, if he did not forthwith return to St. Denys, they fhould iffue a fentence of excommunication againft him; and, at the fame time, the honeft prior, his protector, was very folemnly threatened, that a like cenfure fhould fall on him alfo., if he dared to retain Abeillard any longer in his convent *.

The two friends felt the harfh impreffions of this imperious mandate, but how could it be oppofed? —The abbot, with his monks, returned, and, in a few days, news was brought that heaven had called him to a country, where abbots furrender the enfigns of their dignity, and the humble monk is compelled to obey no longer.

Suger, a name of high renown in the annals of French hiftory, was chofen fucceffor to Adam, in the abbacial honors of St. Denys. He had

* Hift. Calam.

entered very young into the conventual profeſſion, had been educated, in company with Lewis, ſon to Philip the firſt, in the convent of St. Denys; and when the prince came to the throne in 1108, he was called to court, where he became the friend and the counſellor of his maſter. At this time, he was abſent from the kingdom, on an embaſſy to Callixtus the ſecond, pope of Rome, and was returning home, when a meſſenger from St. Denys informed him, that his abbot was dead, and that he was choſen to ſucceed him['].

Abeillard was delighted with the news of this promotion: he could look for every indulgence from the liberal and beneficent character of Suger. The biſhop of Meaux had alſo declared himſelf his friend, and with him he waited in perſon on the new abbot. They expreſſed their ſincere gratulations on the occaſion; and then Abeillard preſented the ſame petition, which had been before rejected. Suger, though a man of the world and condeſcending in his diſpoſitions, was not, however, blind to what he deemed the intereſt of his abbey. The propoſal made to him he could not comply with; he ſaw it in the light it had appeared to others but he obligingly permitted his petitioner: to return to Provins, requeſting he would revolve the important matter more

' Fleury, vol. xiv.

ſeriouſly in his mind, and that he would not think of quitting a houſe, which held his abilities in eſteem, and admired his virtues. The philoſopher was little flattered by the courtly addreſs of his abbot, and he took his leave, reſolute not to deſiſt from a ſcheme, on which his happineſs ſeemed ſo much to depend. He was adviſed to convey his petition to the foot of the throne*.

There was then in the court of Lewis, a very favorite nobleman, Stephen de Garlande, who held the firſt offices about the crown, and whoſe intereſt was irreſiſtible. This man engaged to befriend Abeillard; nor could his cauſe be in better hands. When Suger came next to court, de Garlande took him aſide: "And what motive, "ſaid he to him, can impel you to detain "Abeillard, among you, againſt his free conſent? "The auſterity of his manners does, by no means, "agree with the temper of your convent: his "reproaches bring diſgrace upon you, even in "the eye of the world; and where is the advantage "in poſſeſſing ſuch a ſubject? Believe me, "diſmiſs him, Suger; and think yourſelves "happy to be freed, upon ſuch eaſy terms, "from a man, who is, and ever will be, a "galling thorn in your ſides." -- There was an artful policy in this advice, which Suger ſeems not to have penetrated: De Garlande and

* Hiſt. Calam.

the courtiers apprehended, that Abeillard, who, they knew, was inceffantly inveighing againft the undifciplined lives of the monks, might perhaps fo far fucceed as to give a check to their exceffes. This they wifhed not to fee. In its prefent ftate, St. Denys was more dependent on the will of his majefty, who, by threats of a reform, could at any time draw from them what fums, the exigencies of his crown, or the extravagances of his favorites, were difpofed to call for['].

Suger, when he underftood that it was the will of his mafter that Abeillard fhould be releafed, was too experienced a courtier to oppofe it any longer. He gave his confent, but on fuch terms as he was yet free to prefcribe. The parting with fo great a man, he knew, would reflect difgrace on his abbey. Abeillard therefore, he faid, might quit St. Denys, provided he would be fatisfied to retire to fome lonely wildernefs, and never fubject himfelf to the rule of any other religious inftitute. By this claufe, he conceived, the honor of his houfe would be maintained: it could not be faid that he had left it in queft of higher honors, or in queft of a perfection which might in fome other convent be found, and St. Denys had not to give. In the prefence of the king, thefe conditions were formally fubfcribed to by both parties; and Abeillard, once more was at liberty.

['] Hift. Calam.

Stephen de Garlande, on this occasion the friend of Abeillard, was a man as extraordinary in his fortune, as he was in his character. When very young, and not yet in holy orders, ignorant, dissipated, and debauched, he was elected to the episcopal see of Beauvais; but the pope refused to ratify his nomination. He did not however quit the church, wherein he soon after received the order of deacon, and by his wonderful address making his way to the affections of the king, he rose to the high office of chancellor of the realm. On the death of William, his elder brother, he succeeded to the charge of Senefchal, which was then the post of the greatest honor and power in the French court, comprising in itself, what were afterwards the distinct offices of grand master of the household and of constable. Stephen wore his high honors with splendor; but he wanted sense and moderation to rein his ambition and the native pride of his heart. So great was the ascendency he held over his master's dispositions, that it was sometimes said that Stephen, rather than Lewis, wielded the sceptre of France. With too much appearance of sovereignty, he aimed to extend this control also, over the queen his mistress. She opposed his wild pretensions; when the intoxicated favorite, who no longer prescribed limits to his insolence, dared publicly to insult her. He did not reflect, that an irritated woman is a dangerous enemy.

Adelaide watched the favorable moment, and
reprefented to the king, " that Stephen, the
" proud minifter of his court , was become
" intolerable to the nobles of his realm, and that
" the people , worn down by his oppreffions,
" would fubmit no longer ; that to behold an
" ecclefiaftic , fometimes at the head of armies,
" and then difcharging the civil offices of the
" ftate, was a circumftance which raifed general
" fcandal and difguft; that fhe herfelf could not
" brook his haughty and infultive demeanour;
" and that to her hufband fhe muft now fly for
" protection againft the tyranny of a man , who
" could , at every moment, forget the duties,
" he owed to her rank and dignity ; but that
" there was another circumftance , which came
" nearer to her heart than all this : Lewis,
" continued fhe , in the favors you fhower down
" upon de Garlande , you forget yourfelf: are
" you fenfible that the prince , who delegates
" his effential prerogatives to a minifter , tears
" from his own brow that facred character, which
" gives him refpect in the eye of the multitude."—
The forcible addrefs had its defired effect. The
king fent an order to de Garlande inftantly to
furrender into his hands all the infignia of office,
and to retire from court.

He did retire; but he refufed to refign his charge
of Senefchal , which was become hereditary, he

said, in his family, and he flew to arms. In a
moment the kingdom was in a ferment; Stephen
rode from province to province, and thousands
joined his standard. De Montfort, who had
married his niece, preſſed the king to reinſtate
him in his honors; but in vain. Henry of
England engaged in the quarrel, and Theobald of
Champagne was on his march to ſuccour the fallen
favorite. However, the good fortune of Lewis
prevailed, and de Garlande was reduced to
ſubmiſſion. The queen, alarmed by the troubles,
which innocently ſhe had excited, interceded
for peace. Some time after, Stephen was again
taken into favor, and new honors were conferred
upon him. Thus, in the tranquil enjoyment of
dignity, he ſpent ſome years, when he retired
voluntarily from the ſcene, and died dean of the
chapter of Orleans, the mitre of which he had
refuſed [*].

It was but a dreary proſpect, which Abeillard
had before him, when, agreeably to the conditions
he had ſigned, he left St. Denys. He was poor;
and was he ſure he ſhould find friends who would
be diſpoſed to relieve him? Penury, however,
he conſidered, with all its attendant evils, was
far preferable to the diſguſting enormities of the
abbey, he had left behind him; and having

Abeillard re-
tires into the
foreſt of No-
gent.

[*] Daniel. t. iii. Vie d'Abeil. p. 223.

experienced how little his difpofitions were calculated to coalefce with folly, and how many were
the torments, which fociety fupplied, his
mind began to warm with the refleclion, and he
flattered himfelf that the happinofs, perhaps,
which hitherto he had fought for in vain, might
be found at a diftance from the habitations of men.
Thus penfively he purfued his journey.

As formerly he had wandered through the forefts
of Champagne, he had obferved a fpot, the
recolleclion of which now returned upon his
mind. It was a fmall fequeftered vale, furrounded
by a wood, not diftant from Nogent-fur-Seine,
and a rivulet ran near its fide. It did not appear
that the foot of any mortal had hitherto difturbed
its folitude. To this place Abeillard haftened,
and he fpent his firft night, as did the other tenants
of the foreft, protected only by the wide branches
which fpread over his head. Heloifa fays, it was,
at that time, the receptacle of wild beafts,
and the retreat of robbers; that it had not feen
the habitations of men, or known the charms of
domeftic life[*]. — He had one companion, who
was an ecclefiaftic.

Abeillard, delighted with the novelty of his
fituation, (for when the mind is warmed by a
degree of enthufiafm, it can difcover beauties in a

[*] Ep. Heloif. I[*].

wilderneſs,) waited on the owners of the land, and expreſſed to them his wiſhes of becoming an inhabitant of their woods. The undertaking was then no unuſual thing; and they very freely gave their conſent, and even made him a preſent of any extent of ſoil, he might chuſe to occupy. — The philoſopher returned, and had ſoon meaſured out the diſtrict, which could bound his deſires. — His next ſtep was to apply to the biſhop of Troyes, in whoſe dioceſe his new poſſeſſions lay, for permiſſion to build a ſmall oratory. This likewiſe was granted. — Without loſs of time, Abeillard then and his companion, planned the new building, and with the ſame hands began to erect it. The materials were not diſtant, nor was great ſkill required to put them together. They collected ſome bows of trees; theſe they tied with twigs; and the ſtructure roſe viſibly into form before their eyes. — Having completed what they called their oratory, and ſolemnly dedicated it to the holy Trinity, to expreſs his diſapprobation of the unitarian ſyſtem, which his enemies had alſo imputed to him, they conſtructed a ſecond building, which was to be their own dwelling. This, it may be preſumed, was not more highly finiſhed than the temple they had dedicated to their maker[19].

Seldom had Abeillard been more happy than at this buſy moment. Free from anxious cares, his

[19] Hiſt. Calam.

mind enjoyed the present object. It was not
brilliant indeed ; but it occupied him. He had
escaped from troubles ; the voice of malevolence
sounded no longer in his ears; and persecution
ceased to oppress him. It was the situation of a
weary traveller, who, at the end of his journey,
lays down his heavy burden, and feels contented,
because the load, which pressed him to the earth,
is taken from his shoulders. — Abeillard rose with
the sun to adore his maker; he thanked him for
the repose he enjoyed, and he lamented the follies
of his life. The day he spent in study, or in
conversation with his friend, to whom he recounted
the adventures and the perils he had gone through.
The water of the brook allayed his thirst, and
of the very scanty provisions, which the forests of
Champagne could supply, he made his meal.
With the birds, which sang round him, he
retired to rest : and he laid his head down on
the turf, careless and undisturbed. — A mind,
like his, could, not indeed circumscribe itself
within the precincts of his lonely habitation: it
would range the ideal world; enter there into
active scenes; and sometimes perhaps be pleased
with the prospect of future honors and renown.
But foresee he could not, that this career of glory
was ready to open in the very wilderness, which
seemed to have put an eternal bar to the familiar
intercourse of mortals.

When

When it was publicly known, that Abeillard was again an independent man, and had feceded entirely from the world, the lovers of science, and many who had before been his fcholars, inquired anxioufly for his abode, refolved, could the learned folitary be difcovered, to put themfelves under his tuition, and once more to draw fcience from his lips. Their fearch was foon crowned with fuccefs: they found him fituated, as I have defcribed, in the foreft near Nogent; and they opened their wifhes to him.—Abeillard in vain refifted; he faw every avenue to his hermitage filling with young men, and crowds were round him, before he had time to take the advice of friends, or to confult the feelings of his own heart. The ftep could not at firft feem pleafing, unlefs already the pure delights of folitude had begun to pall upon his mind. With one voice they requefted, he would again become their mafter. He fhowed them his humble cell, the oratory he had raifed, and he pointed to the wildernefs, which their eager fteps had juft penetrated. " Your propofal, faid he to them, is " inconfiderate. I can but applaud your thirft after " knowledge; and the choice you make of me " for an inftructer, is truly flattering. But you " forget yourfelves. In a moment, this dreary " fpot will teach you, that fcience, without the ·

" conveniences of life, is not worth purfuing ".".
— His remonftrance was to little purpofe : when
the mind is ftrongly bent to an object, the
view of ordinary difficulties does but animate its
exertions.

" If want of conveniences, faid they, be the
" obftacle which ftands in our way, we will foon
" remove it."— An extraordinary interefting fcene
now commenced. They looked round them,
when, after a fhort conference, it was determined
that, in imitation of Abeillard, they fhould
become their own architects, and provide, in the
firft place, againft the inclemencies of the air.
Their mafter's cell gave the general plan. They
tore down branches from the trees, and they
twifted the pliant twigs. In a few hours the
bufinefs was nearly completed. — Abeillard viewed,
with infinite fatisfaction, the bufy fcene; his
approbation gave frefh life to their exertions; and
it was no longer poffible he could refufe his affent
to a petition, which was pronounced with fuch
unqueftionable marks of fincerity".".

He came forward : they read confent in his
looks: " With to-morrow's fun, faid he, I will
" meet you under yon fpreading tree, and with
" the bleffing of heaven on my endeavours, what
" inftructions it may be in my power to give you,
" you fhall freely receive from me." They heard
his words with general acclamations.

" Hift. Calm.   " Vie d'Abeil. 233.

The wants of nature now called for attention; but when the mind, engroffed with its own thoughts, retires in upon itfelf, thefe calls are eafily fatisfied. They, whom the luxurious tables of Paris could hardly gratify, now fat down to roots, and they found them favoury. The oaten cake had a relifh, which they had not experienced in the ortolan. Their beds were made of dry weeds, or of the leaves which had fallen from the trees ".—Thus did this new tribe of philofophers prepare themfelves for the approach of wifdom: the academic grove was truly feen to rife again, and never had the ancient fages on whofe praifes hiftory dwells with wonder, fought for truth with more ardent inquiries. — Abeillard pronounced his firft lecture: it was from the foot of the tree, I mentioned: his hearers were feated round; for they had made themfelves benches of bows, and had raifed the green turf into tables ".

I have before remarked how extraordinary was this thirft after knowledge, which, with a degree of enthufiafm, of which we can form no idea, fpread itfelf over the ftates of Europe. But nothing can mark more ftrongly the fallen condition of literature. When learned men are common, and learning itfelf is very generally diffufed, not only the means of acquiring it are at hand, but

" Hift. Calam. " Ibid.

there is alfo no novelty in the purfuit, calculated
to excite peculiar energy and to roufe the paffions.
In the times I am defcribing, a learned man was
a phenomenon; and who can be furprifed that
he fhould have been viewed with wonder? What
is rare is highly prized ; and what we prize is
fought for, fometimes with an eagernefs which
aftonifhes cooler minds, and before which obftacles
either vanifh, or only ferve to give an additional
fpring to exertions. — The fcarcity of books,
before the invention of printing, was likewife
another principal circumftance, which, as it
circumfcribed the fpread of learning, fo did it
render thofe, who, furmounting every impediment,
attained it, objects of greater admiration.

Before the end of the firft year, the number
of Abeillard's fcholars exceeded fix hundred,
fituated in a foreft, fuch as I have defcribed,
expofed to the inclement feafons, without a fingle
convenience to fmooth the rugged life, or without
one amufement, excepting what literary purfuits,
fcientific converfation, and their own fociety could
fupply. — The fubjects they difcuffed were either
philofophical or religious, to which Abeillard
added differtations on the moral and focial duties,
which he could enliven by the brilliancy of his
imagination, and by anecdotes drawn from facred
and profane hiftory. But it matters little, as I
have elfewhere obferved, what our purfuits be,

provided they excite attention, and we place our interest in them. — The compositions indeed of Abeillard I can read with little pleasure; they are jejune, intricate, and inelegant; and to me such would have been his lectures. I could not have inhabited the Champagne forests, nor have travelled in quest of such literary lore; and my European contemporaries will not dissent from me: but this only shows that, with circumstances, our dispositions vary, and that nothing can be more irrational, than to measure by the same standard, the notions and characters of two ages so remote, as this and the twelfth century.

Abeillard, as it may be collected from his memoirs, at their hours of recreation, talked to his scholars of the ancient philosophers; he told them how these sages lived; he recounted the purity of their manners, and the eminence of their virtues: he turned to the sacred volumes, which relate the lives of the sons of the prophets; and here he found men who, near the waters of Jordan, had emulated the perfection of angels. With rapture he dwelt on the more than mortal virtues of the Baptist, and he followed the first converts to christianity through their exemplary course of self-abasement, of prayer, of recollection, and of temperance. With these splendid epochs he compared the present day. They listened with complacency. In Abeillard they saw the divine Plato: and in

BOOK
IV.

themfelves that illuftrious group of difciples,
which had given renown to the academic walks of
Athens.

But the ferenity of the fky began to cloud over.
His enemies heard, with indignation, of the
fuccefs of his labors, and of the new honors
which attended him in the wildernefs. Should
this be unoppofed; in what could it terminate,
but in their own difgrace, and in the further
exaltation of Abeillard? Impatiently they looked
to fome event, which, from the character of their
rival, or in the probable courfe of things, could
not, they trufted, be very diftant: this they would
feize, and once more attempt his downfal.

He builds the
Paraclet.

In the mean while, this learned colony daily
increafed and profpered more. But as the firft
enthufiafm abated, they could feel more fenfibly
the inconveniences, to which the inhofpitable
fituation expofed them: thefe they now wifhed to
remove, and to bring round them fome few, at
leaft, of the comforts of domeftic life. They
wanted not means, if they would turn them to
advantage; and they could even command what
fums of money might be neceffary, if expenfe
were called for. Their mafter was deftitute of every
thing; and for the intellectual treafures he fupplied,
were they to make no return? Neceffaries, at leaft,
their own hands could give him: they improved

his cell, they tilled his field, they dreſſed his
victuals, and they clothed him. — "My penury,
" ſays he of himſelf, was at that time extreme:
" but I could not dig, and to beg I was aſhamed.
" Recurring therefore to the profeſſion, I beſt
" underſtood, I made my tongue execute, what
" my hands were unfit for [17]."

They then undertook to enlarge their place of
worſhip; and they propoſed doing it, on a more
improved and permanent plan. Stones and timber
were prepared ; and from theſe they erected a
building, inelegant indeed, but firm and reſpect-
able. The firſt humble ſtructure, as I mentioned,
was dedicated to the ſacred Trinity. Now, in
ſolemn ceremony , Abeillard and his diſciples
aſſembled : he explained to them the motives,
which had induced him to prefer that myſterious
name; and he added that, as he had entered this
deſert, funk down with care, where the goodneſs
of heaven had watched over him, and he had
found comfort , could he more emphatically
expreſs his gratitude, than by conſecrating this more
auguſt temple to that perſon of the holy triad,
which more peculiarly is ſtyled the Comforter?
" We will dedicate it, ſaid he, to the Pa-
" raclet [18]."

The circumſtances of this event, Heloiſa thus
relates: " On the very dens of wild beaſts, and

[17] Hiſt. Calam.   [18] Ibid.

" on the lurking holes of thieves, where the name
" of God had not been heard, you raised a
" temple to his name, and you confecrated it to
" his holy fpirit. To this the donations of kings
" or princes did not contribute; you wanted not
" their aid. From all quarters, an almoft infinite
" number of fcholars crowded to be inftructed
" by you. They fupplied whatever was neceffary.
" Even churchmen, who had been ufed to live
" on the donations of others, whofe hands were
" ever open to receive, but not to give, became
" here profufe ; they were importunate in their
" contributions ".."

Great offence was taken by the zealots, when
it was known, that Abeillard had dedicated his
oratory to the Paraclet. It had not been heard,
that any building had hitherto been put under the
protection of that myfterious fpirit. The Reimifh
profeffors were paticularly loud: but it was a
circumftance, they thought, which, if properly
managed, might be turned to advantage. — When
nothing ferioufly reprehenfible, in the conduct or
the belief of an adverfary, can be detected, the
mereft trifle will be made matter of cenfure;
efpecially any novelty in opinion or language will
be noticed as a crime, on which malevolence,
with wonderful rancor, will love to faften. — A
church, thefe wife cafuifts fagacioufly obferved,

" Ep. Helois, 1ª.

might be dedicated to the Son or to the Holy Trinity, but not to the Father, nor to the Holy Spirit. — Abeillard, who should have smiled at the puerile nonsense, seemed seriously affected: he knew indeed the temper of his adversaries, and he very gravely undertook to justify what he had done, by arguments from scripture and reason. — To reason with such men was telling them that their observations merited notice : they would only repeat them with more inveteracy : ridicule is sometimes the best test of truth.

But the professors, it seems, were rather conscious of some weakness: they did not chuse to expose themselves alone in a controversy, which might require more than their own address to give it consequence: they had recourse to foreign aid. "Sensible, says Abeillard, that their own "powers could not go far, they took care to "instigate against me two new apostles, in whom "the world then much confided. The one boasted "that he had revived the spirit of the ancient "canons ; and the other that of the monks. "These men, roaming about the earth, by "their impudent invectives, rendered me contemp- "tible in the eyes not only of the ecclesiastical, "but also of some secular powers. The reports, "they circulated, of my conduct and religious "tenets, alienated the affections of my best friends; "and the few, who still retained the smallest kindness

Norbert of
Premontré.

" for me, awed by the names of my opponents,
" judged it beft to conceal their fentiments". —
The one of thefe was Norbert of Premontré, and
the other the famous Bernard of Clairvaux.

St. Norbert, defcended from an illuftrious
German family, was born in the dutchy of
Cleves. When young, he was called to the
court of the emperor, Henry the fifth, his
relation. Here, the elegance of his manners,
the affability of his temper, and the general
charms of his deportment, gained him uncommon
admiration. But what contributed to fafhion his
exterior, infenfibly corrupted his heart: he became diffipated and licentious. The danger, to
which his life was, one day, expofed from a
violent ftorm of thunder, roufed him to refleftion:
he withdrew from the court, refigned his
employments, fold his eftates, and diftributed
his riches among the poor. Thus difengaged from
every tie, which united him to the world, he
began a fevere courfe of penance: but the mortifica-
tions he thought expedient for himfelf, he wifhed
to inculcate to others. He preached to the
neighbouring people; from them he carried his
inftruftions to more diftant provinces, and the
fuccefs which attended his labors was great. His
fcheme of introducing a general reform, particularly
among churchmen, was violently oppofed: he met
enemies at every ftep.

" Hift. Calam.

In 1118 he waited on pope Gelafius, who was in France, from whom he obtained an unbounded permiffion to preach, fuch as had been granted to Robert d'Arbriffelles. Two years afterwards he was prevailed on to make fome ftay at Laon, by his friend, the bifhop of that city. He offered him for his retreat a neighbouring valley. Norbert was delighted with the folitary fpot: it was called *Premontré:* and here he laid the foundation of that reformed order, which has taken its name from the vale. The cares of his rifing family did not however confine him at home; he continued his former preaching, and travelled much[19]. — At this period it was that, inftigated by the mifreprefentations of the enemies of Abeillard, he made the philofopher, with whom he was not particularly acquainted, a fubject of public reprehenfion.

The zeal of good men is often too irritable. Norbert was not very learned, and he would eafily be impofed on by fuch men as Albericus and Lotulphus. — The wandering faint, in 1126, was chofen archbifhop of Magdeburgh.

Bernard, the reflorer of monaftic difcipline in the Weftern church, the engine, which gave life and energy to the religion and politics of Europe, the thaumatergus of the twelfth century, was born, in 1091, near Dijon, in Burgundy, of an ancient and noble family. His mother,

Bernard of Clairvaux.

[19] Fleury, vol. xiv.

agreeably to the romantic piety of the age, awed
by a dream, devoted him, in a particular manner,
to the fervice of God, whilst fhe bore him in
her womb. He was the third of fix fons. Nature
had endowed him with uncommon abilities, and
his education was fitted to his high deftination.
He loved retirement, he reflected much, and he
fpoke little, at a time, when youth is moft forward
and exuberant. He was fimple in his manners,
mild in converfation, and modeft as angelic
innocence. The beauty of his perfon accorded
with the elegance of his mind: there was a harmony
in his voice which captivated, his language was
perfpicuous, and eloquence, in fweeteft accents
fell, like honey, from his lips. — He entered
the world, and every object feemed to fmile at
his appearance: ambition, fcience, pleafure, at
once laid their charms at his feet. But Bernard
could not be feduced. The world he faw was a
perilous ocean; and fo peculiar was his caft of
mind, that vice, in whatever form it prefented itfelf,
only ftruck him with horror. Very foon the placid
current of his thoughts was ruffled: in vain he ftrove
to oppofe the diffipation which, at every turn, met
his eye; the counteraction of his foul was vehement; and he felt an enthufiafm ftir within him,
to which, till now, he had been a ftranger.

The pleafing emotion, which this dangerous
paffion excites, has a thoufand charms; becaufe

though it pictures vice in the most horrid and disgusting forms, it, at the same time, represents virtue with every alluring feature: religion seems to hold before it its most exclusive blessings, and heaven, in all its glories, bursts upon the sight. But as the passions, which are styled the springs of life, are only serviceable, so long as they continue under the check of reason, and are ever, from their natural tendency, running to excess; so is religious enthusiasm of all passions the most dangerous: it takes its rise in excess, and is only ruled by impulse; it begins by hating vice, and soon carries its hatred to the vicious; to itself it takes the rewards of virtue and the promises of revelation, and to others it extends the judgments of heaven in this life, and its vindictive punishments in the next. — Bernard resolved to turn his back on a world, which only gave him disgust, and which he could not reform.

Citeaux, in Burgundy, the first monastery of the Cistercian order, had been founded fifteen years: but the rule they had adopted was so severe, that very few had yet chosen to submit themselves to its austerities. It was to this institute that young Bernard turned his eyes: its rigid discipline seemed to harmonize with the state of his mind. His friends strenuously opposed the design, and they endeavoured to avert his attention. It was in vain: enthusiasm is not conquered by oppofition. Rather his refolution daily gained ftrength: the call of heaven feemed to found in his ears, and to charge him with indolence. — More than once he had experienced the efficacy of his own oratory, and he might fufpect that the religious glow, which animated his own heart, could be communicated to others. In his defign he was irrevocably fixed ; but if he could take his friends along with him, it would be a glorious at- chievement, and the facrifice to heaven would be more complete. He undertook it, and fucceeded.

Awed into fubmiffion by a perfuafive ftrain of eloquence, which was irrififtible, to the aid of which he, at every turn, called heaven and its judgments, four of his brothers joined him in his undertaking; and very foon the number of his followers increafed to thirty. This powerful reinforcement he conducted to Citeaux. — Bernard was, at this time, in his twenty-fecond year.

As he had withdrawn from the world, to be forgotten by it, and to bury himfelf in folitude ; his firft ftep was to banifh every fentiment, which could tie him to fociety or to the earth. The maftery he acquired over his fenfes was aftonifhing : abforbed in the contemplation of heavenly things, he rofe above the impreffions of matter, and was truly a fpiritual man. Having never indulged his paffions, they could have no fway over him : he only ate to fupport nature, and he flept, when his head, through laſſitude, ſank to the earth. To ſuch inceſſant auſterities the delicacy of his conſtitution gave way: like to a flower, cut by the mower's ſithe, his health languiſhed, his beauty withered, and he ſeemed to bend to the grave. But the vigor of his mind abated not, and the fervor of his devotion only grew into greater animation. It was neceſſary to check this ardent career, and the authority of ſuperiors interpoſed.

In 1115, Clairvaux was founded, and Bernard, though but beginning the ſecond year of his religious life, was nominated abbot. His brothers went along with him. In this new poſt, where example was neceſſary to animate his followers, the young abbot exhibited freſh inſtances of his unbounded fervor. Clairvaux was a barren ſpot: the monks labored, and tilled its ſurface, but it only returned weeds, or a few weak and inſipid vegetables. On theſe they lived. Bernard, in the retirement of his cell, converſed with angels: when he came out among his brethren, a heavenly brightneſs appeared to radiate from his countenance; he ſpoke of things, which they did not comprehend; and when he preſcribed rules of conduct, or deſcanted on religious perfection, it ſeemed that he had forgotten, that his hearers were mortal. They liſtened with amazement; they admired his maxims; but they felt their weakneſs, and could only wiſh to practiſe what he taught.

As the fame of his fanctity fpread, he was vifited from all quarters, and the filence of his retirement was broken. The affairs of his convent alfo, and fometimes the concerns of others, drew him into the world. Wherever he went, curiofity affembled thoufands round him. He preached to them, laying before them the delights of folitude; and he returned to his cell, followed by innumerable profelytes, whom his eloquence had converted. — Now it was, as his hiftorians relate, that nature began to be obedient to his voice; and the number of miracles, he is faid to have worked, are recorded by them with veneration and aftonifhment.

Miracles. I am ready to believe that Bernard, whom his difciples and the multitude viewed as a prodigy, and as the peculiar friend of heaven, might be very capable of producing fuch effects, as, at that time particularly, would be neceffarily conftrued into miraculous operations. It can be denied by no one, who has attended to man; who knows the texture of his frame, the influence of circumftances, and the powers of imagination. — I muft likewife grant, that he, to whofe beck nature and nature's laws are ever obedient, can, when it pleafes him, fufpend their operation, or modify their effects. This, at all times, he has done: and who fhall fay, that he has ceafed from doing it? — But when critically we examine the prodigies,

afcribed

afcribed to Bernard and other holy men, at thefe times of cimmerian darknefs; can we, confiftently with the notions, which modern difcoveries and the improved ftate of fcience fuggeft, attribute them to a real preternatural agency? Had many of them happened, juft as they are told, ftill, I think, they might, on philofophical principles, be accounted for; but it is evident, that their relaters viewed them as wonders, and recorded them as fuch. A hiftorian, under fuch impreffions, would be too much difpofed, even unintentionally, to depart from the fimplicity of honeft narration.

Ignorance, or a heated imagination, which would deceive the incautious fpectator, might alfo impofe on him, who fhould confider himfelf as the minifter of omnipotence. Bernard, for inftance, had heard of the miracles, which his predeceffors or his contemporaries in fanctity had worked, and he had believed them: in fimilar circumftances, an unufual impulfe would feem to move within him, and he would think divine providence was preparing to make ufe of him as an inftrument, of his mercies or of his judgments to man. Such a fentiment would, by no means, be inconfiftent with the moft perfect piety and felf-abafement. — But is it credible that he, who, in infinite wifdom eftablifhed his eternal laws on the fitnefs and univerfal relation of things, would

Q

subvert the divine harmony of his syſtem, unleſs a criſis, worthy of it, ſhould intervene? I do not find this criſis in the vulgar hiſtory of the miracles of the dark ages.

When a new religion, ſuch as the chriſtian, was to be founded or propagated, extraordinary means would be ſometimes neceſſary. Incredulity, rivetted on habits and the ſtrong oppoſition of inveterate prejudices, was to be ſurmounted; and it was expedient that the miſſion of him, who delivered a new and unheard of doctrine, ſhould be eſtabliſhed on an authority, which nothing might controvert.— In the times of Bernard, was there an object, like this, in agitation? Or rather, is not he ſaid to have worked miracles, the general importance of which cannot be diſcovered; for they regard private intereſts, perſonal views, and ſometimes, it appears, rather unimportant matters. — A man of family and his relation had ſuddenly loſt his ſpeech and his recollection. His friends were afflicted, that he ſhould die without confeſſion and the rites of the church, and they came to Bernard. The ſaint aſſured them that, if ſatisfaction were made to the church and the poor, which the nobleman had pillaged and oppreſſed, he ſhould recover, and be in a ſituation to confeſs his ſins. They agreed to the conditions. Bernard then fell on his knees; when news was brought him, that the ſick man had recovered his ſpeech.

He then made his confeſſion to the faint, performed other works of piety, and died after three days[20].
— Let this miracle, which was wonderfully celebrated, as the firſt which the faint worked, be tried by the received canons of impartial criticiſm.

It is remarkable that, in proportion as the clouds of ignorance have diſperſed, as ſcience has diffuſed its benign influence, and as religion has been purified from the baſe allay of human opinions, thoſe portentous events have ceaſed to happen. The circumſtance, it muſt be owned, is not favorable to the credit of our pious anceſtors. Why ſhould providence with-hold his preternatural interference at a time, mankind is beſt able to appreciate the wondrous ſyſtem of his ways, and would be moſt diſpoſed to honor them? Ignorance, ſuperſtition, bigotry, and enthuſiaſm, have, moſt clearly, attended the progreſs of miraculous operations, through that long ſeries of years, when their appearance was thought to be moſt frequent. — Many, I know, of thoſe events might, in a certain ſenſe, be termed miraculous, becauſe they exceeded the powers of nature, as theſe were then underſtood. Carry back into the twelfth century, the aſtoniſhing effects of animal magnetiſm, or the reſuſcitations, which almoſt daily take place, of perſons apparently dead by drowning or ſuffocation, what aſtoniſhment would be excited!

[20] Fleury, vol. xiv.

Q 2

Ignorant of such caufes which, in the regular
courfe of things, could produce the effect; to
what could they have recourfe but to preternatural agency? And they would be juftified in the
judgment, they might form. On us it is incumbent
to be more cautious: with the accuracy of inquiry
we weigh modern events, proportioning caufes to
affects, we fhould meafure thofe of our more
credulous, becaufe lefs informed, anceflors.

The author of miracles is likewife the author of
nature : nor is he more admirable, when he
departs from eftablifhed order, than when, uniformly
omnipotent, he conducts, with unerring rectitude,
the vaft fyftem of the univerfe. The general ways
of providence are to me more awful and fublime,
becaufe they proceed on plans, which infinite
wifdom projected and fupports: but in miraculous
events, which to us are deordinations, that fame
providence, out of compaffion to human weaknefs,
defcends from his fphere of incomprehenfible
greatnefs, and deigns to fpeak to our fenfes a
language, which may over-awe reafon, and command an involuntary affent. Had man been more
perfect than he is, the intervention of miracles
would have been unneceffary: they are no compliment to the powers of human intellect.

It was, when the reputation of Bernard was
high, and he began to draw himfelf from folitude

He then made his confeſſion to the ſaint, performed other works of piety, and died after three days". — Let this miracle, which was wonderfully celebrated, as the firſt which the ſaint worked, be tried by the received canons of impartial criticiſm.

It is remarkable that, in proportion as the clouds of ignorance have diſperſed, as ſcience has diffuſed its benign influence, and as religion has been purified from the baſe allay of human opinions, thoſe portentous events have ceaſed to happen. The circumſtance, it muſt be owned, is not favorable to the credit of our pious anceſtors. Why ſhould providence with-hold his preternatural interference at a time, mankind is beſt able to appreciate the wondrous ſyſtem of his ways, and would be moſt diſpoſed to honor them? Ignorance, ſuperſtition, bigotry, and enthuſiaſm, have, moſt clearly, attended the progreſs of miraculous operations, through that long ſeries of years, when their appearance was thought to be moſt frequent. — Many, I know, of thoſe events might, in a certain ſenſe, be termed miraculous, becauſe they exceeded the powers of nature, as theſe were then underſtood. Carry back into the twelfth century, the aſtoniſhing effects of animal magnetiſm, or the reſuſcitations, which almoſt daily take place, of perſons apparently dead by drowning or ſuffocation, what aſtoniſhment would be excited!

" Fleury, vol. xiv.   Q 2

Ignorant of such causes which, in the regular course of things, could produce the effect; to what could they have recourse but to preternatural agency? And they would be justified in the judgment, they might form. On us it is incumbent to be more cautious: with the accuracy of inquiry we weigh modern events, proportioning causes to effects, we should measure those of our more credulous, because less informed, ancestors.

The author of miracles is likewise the author of nature: nor is he more admirable, when he departs from established order, than when, uniformly omnipotent, he conducts, with unerring rectitude, the vast system of the universe. The general ways of providence are to me more awful and sublime, because they proceed on plans, which infinite wisdom projected and supports: but in miraculous events, which to us are deordinations, that same providence, out of compassion to human weakness, descends from his sphere of incomprehensible greatness, and deigns to speak to our senses a language, which may over-awe reason, and command an involuntary assent. Had man been more perfect than he is, the intervention of miracles would have been unnecessary: they are no compliment to the powers of human intellect.

It was, when the reputation of Bernard was high, and he began to draw himself from solitude

into public obfervation, that Abeillard, whofe
character and habits of thinking had been unfairly
reprefented, became an object of his cenfure.
Bernard was incautioufly betrayed into a vehement
animofity, which is hardly reconcileable with the
upright difpofitions of his mind: means therefore
muft have been ufed as impofing, as they were
ungenerous. The prejudice, he imbibed againft
him, fank deep in his heart, as will be feen in
the continuation of my hiftory.

Abeillard, whom the news of this powerful confederation ftruck with amazement, faw the danger,
to which he was expofed. His heart fank within
him: " God is my witnefs, fays he, as often as I
" was told of any ecclefiaftical meeting, I conceived
" it was affembled againft me; and in trepidation
" I waited the fummons, which would drag me
" to their bar ''."—The remembrance of Soiffons
haunted his recollection, and as he wanted fortitude
to withftand the impreffion, he fell, like a broken
reed, before it. In defpair he meditated the
wildeft plans: he would retire, he thought, from
the confines of the chriftian world; he would feek
refuge among the difciples of Mahomet; where,
under the ftipulation of fuch a tribute, as they
fhould pleafe to impofe, he fhould be at liberty,
he trufted, to lead the life of a chriftian amongft
the enemies of Chrift. When they fhould hear,

'' Hift. Calam.

Q 3

BOOK
IV.

that he had been accused of holding opinions,
adverse to chriflianity, they might be inclined, he
thought, to treat him more gently; they might
even imagine, he could be profelyted to their
belief ".

Loſt in theſe deſponding thoughts, he indulged
the romantic wiſh of expatriating himſelf for ever:
the Paraclet could no longer give him pleaſure;
he ſuſpended his leſſons, his ſcholars in part
withdrew, and nothing but deſolation and the
horrors of the wilderneſs roſe in proſpect before
him. But unexpectedly an event took place, which
promiſed, if not thoroughly to alleviate his misfortunes, at leaſt to break the dark cloud, which
lowered round him. When anxiety preſſes, or
pain, of whatever deſcription, makes life uneaſy,
the moſt trifling variation gives relief.

There was in Little Britany a monaſtery, of very
ancient renown, founded, as it is ſaid, in the fifth
century, by Gildas our countryman, in the reign
of king Childeric, the ſon of Meroveus ". It was
called St. Gildas de Ruys; and the abbot was lately
dead. Abeillard, by the unanimous voice of the
monks, was choſen ſuperior of this houſe, and the
duke of Britany gave his warmeſt approbation to
their choice. The philoſopher, a native of the
province, would be naturally admired by his

' " Hiſt. Calam.   " Notæ Quercet.

countrymen, and they would wish to possess him.
A messenger was sent to St. Denys to beg the consent
of Suger, to whom Abeillard still belonged: his
consent was easily obtained. The deputy then
proceeded into Champagne; where he found
Abeillard in his retirement, abashed and melancholy, and he laid before him the letters of his
promotion, which he had brought from St. Gildas.
The philosopher perused them with the indifference
of a man, who was neither flattered by the prof-
fered honors, nor could augur much happiness to
himself in the event. He paused: his present heart-
breaking situation was to be weighed against the
uncertainty of future prospects.—Should he retire
from the Paraclet; the persecutions, which again
threatened him, would cease perhaps, and he
might be happy: but the land, to which he was
called, was almost barbarous, and their language
was unknown to him: besides, report had told
him, that the monks of St. Gildas were dissipated
and undisciplined; and how much had he not
suffered from this circumstance in the abbey of
St. Denys? But he who sees a naked dagger,
suspended by a hair over his head, would rush
into a precipice to avoid its point.—In a more
favorable view; was not command offered him?
And might he not be able, by the exertion of it,
to repress the bad conduct of his monks, and to
establish his own authority? They might also be

inclined to refpect his learning, his virtue, and his renown.—The laft reflection preponderated, and he anfwered the meffenger, that he was ready to accompany him into Britany[10]. Still, his heart was heavy: he left the Paraclet, committing it to the care of two intimate friends.

Abeillard foon was fenfible how imprudently he had made his choice. He found St. Gildas in a ftate of depravation, of which no idea could have been formed; and he was more than furprifed, that they fhould ever have fixed on him for their fuperior. Their general language was the harfh jargon of the country; and he knew not how to make them fenfible of the enormities of their lives, or of his defign to reform them. The obligations of his charge were however preffing; and though he forefaw the anxiety and dangers, to which it would expofe him, he determined not to neglect his duty. As well might he have attempted to preach virtue to a band of lawlefs robbers.—In aggravation to all this, the lord of the territory, a man of confiderable power, availing himfelf of the notorious conduct of the monks, had not only contrived to fubject the abbey to his control, but had alfo feized fuch of their poffeffions, as pleafed him beft: the whole country groaned under his exactions[11].

[10] Hift. Calam. [11] Ibid.

To diftrefs their abbot, whofe fchemes of reformation they abhorred, the monks importunately
applied to him for clothing and other neceffaries;
though they knew he was deftitute of every
thing. Hitherto they had made their own provifions;
and out of the flock, they could fteal or lay by,
had contrived to fupport themfelves, their concu-
bines, and their fons and daughters. 'More than
ever they were now active to pilfer the common
ftore, that Abeillard, finding it impoffible to
fatisfy their wants, might be forced to with-draw
himfelf from amongft them, or to drop his
taftelefs fcheme of reformation.'[a].

This fituation of Abeillard was really more
diftrefsful, than any he had hitherto experienced.
When he looked round him, he fays, he could
difcover nothing but a moft barbarous and lawlefs
people, from whom nor affiftance, nor advice,
could be expected; their notions and habits of
life were in direct oppofition to his own. If he
quitted the door of his convent, the tyrant, juft
mentioned, or his guards, met his eye; and
their geftures told him that he was their flave. If
he returned home; there was a worfe enemy
waiting within, whofe intemperate clamors founded,
like the fhrieks of difcord, in his ears. He viewed
the harfh decrees of fate, which, with an accelerated

[a] Hift. Calam.

force, feemed to weigh upon him; and if, in rueful defpondency, he lamented, we muft now forgive him. He recollected that, on former occafions, he might have given fome caufe for oppreffion; but that now he was guiltlefs: he recollected that, hitherto it had been at leaft in his power to do fome good by example or inftruction, and therein comfort might be found; but that now every exertion was as ufelefs to himfelf, as it was to others: he recollected all the repofeful moments of the Paraclet, and in the recollection his mind was too fedulous to omit every care, which had really difturbed their ferenity. — " And " could I leave the Paraclet, exclaimed he, that " is, the comforter, to rufh into certain mifery? " I was threatened indeed; but muft I run from " threats, when dangers, I knew, would " inevitably overtake me at every ftep" !" Nor was he a little hurt, that he fhould have left his dear oratory in fo neglected a ftate; that he had not provided for the due celebration of divine fervice: but what could he do, who was poor? Or could a wildernefs make up the deficiencies of penury?

At this time, Suger, abbot of St. Denys, whofe power was great in the court of Lewis the fixth, thinking the moment favorable for the completion of a fcheme, which he had for fome time agitated,

[11] Hift. Calam.

affembled the chapter of his convent, and laid his defign before them. He had difcovered in fome old writings of his abbey, that Argenteuil, where Heloifa, as the reader will recollect, refided, belonged in ftrict juftice to St. Denys. This right he refolved to urge, whilft he had power in his hands, which could give it efficacy. The chapter applauded his defign. Without delay deputies were fent to Rome, vefted with ample authority, and they carried with them fuch papers, as were requifite, to eftablifh the ground of their pretenfions. — In addition to this right, which was weak in itfelf, and by prefcription obfolete[11], Suger was in poffeffion of another plea, in which probably he confided moft. The nuns of Argenteuil, if there be truth in his reprefentation, were diffolute and worldly-minded : this circum- ftance, with all the glow of defcription, was to be laid before the Roman pontiff. Could he obtain his requeft, he affured Honorius, that, where vice and diffipation now prevailed, he would introduce, with his monks, a fyftem of reform, which fhould do honor to the monaftic inftitute. — It is remarkable that Suger, who could not be ignorant of the enormities, with which his own houfe was charged, fhould have the effrontery to infift on arguments, which muft

---

[11] Notæ Quercet.

necessarily bring reprehension on himself. The
negociation however succeeded, and Argenteuil,
with all its appendages, was solemnly made over
to the abbey of St. Denys. The king, whom Suger
calls his master and his friend, confirmed the
donation about the year 1127 [11].

Heloisa was priorefs, that is, second in office,
when this unploafant event happened. I am
willing to hope, though she was involved in the
general accufation, that she was innocent of the
crimes, with which Argentcuil was charged.
Abeillard relates the fact, I have mentioned;
but he only speaks of the pretended right, on
which Suger founded his claim. Nor do I think
that, either love for Heloisa, or a general feeling
for her sisters, would have with-held his pen,
had he known them to be guilty in the degree
some historians reprefent: they take their accounts
from Suger.

The lovely priorefs had been seven years in
confinement: to the historian they are seven years
of silence. His imagination, indeed, is free to
delineate her actions and her gentle turn of
character, as fancy may direct; but had the
regular feries of her employments been minutely
recorded, it would have afforded little indulgence
to curiofity. The life of a nun is uniformly compofed
of a thousand little actions and trifling incidents;

[11] Suger, de reb. a se geft.

and the hiflory of one day may be efteemed the hiflory of her life. Heloifa, we may prefume, wore away her days in prayer, in ftudy, in converfation, in retirement: but if the conduct of the fiflerhood was fuch, as Suger tells, the want of difcipline would allow her more room for the indulgence of her own peculiar difpofitions, and their exceffes might difturb her little. She had entered Argenteuil, we know, with great reluctance, though in perfect fubmiffion to the will of Abeillard : if therefore her heart but flowly bent itfelf to the maxims of a reclufe, it was but natural. Her fortitude was great; but the example, which furrounded her, was ill-adapted to prepare her foul for the ingrefs of divine grace, or rather perhaps of that amiable enthufiafm, which can give fweetnefs to folitude and to the many little practices, which form the tiffue, and conftitute the almoft effential character of the monaftic life.

It was in this houfe fhe had received the rudiments of thofe literary accomplifhments, which, in a dark age, rendered her a prodigy of fcience. The fame means would afterwards fupply her more abundant occafions of improvement; and doubtlefs fhe availed herfelf of them. She had liftlefs hours to fill up, fhe had anxious cares to remove, fhe had the unavailing thoughts of a lover to reprefs, and fhe had a heavy heart to cheer,

It was well she could find any employment, which might anfwer thefe important ends, and which could occupy her attention. But the idea of Abeillard, as I fhall have ample occafion to remark, had fo modified her heart, that it feems to have been affociated with the motion of every fibre, which compofed it.

Heloifa goes to the Pa- raclet. Suger having obtained the grant, he fo anxioufly wifhed, (for Argenteuil was, at that time, a very opulent eflablifhment,) was not flow in bringing it to execution. He fent a peremptory order to the nuns; commanding them to furrender their convent into his hands, and he fignified to them the authorities, on which he proceeded. They refufed to obey; when force was employed, and they were violently ejedled[10]. — It is faid, that Suger had figned an agreement, whereby he promifed to provide for the fupport of the nuns: and part of the community, it is known, was received into a neighbouring convent[11]. But Heloifa, with a few companions, was thrown on the world, without fuccour and without friends.

Abeillard was at St. Gildas, forlorn as I defcribed him, when he heard of this event. However felfifh he might be, he could not but feel for the fituation of Heloifa; and on his mind hung another thought, which would piompt him to be more adlive in her fervice. I have faid, that he was

[10] Hift. Calam. [11] Notæ Querect.

much attached to the Paraclet, and that he lamented, he had been obliged to leave it in fo neglected a condition. Now did an occafion prefent itfelf, when he might indulge his partiality for that place; and by fuccouring the diftreffed, he might perhaps alfo be able to raife it even to celebrity, and himfelf to inherit the glory, which belonged to the founders of convents. The idea pleafed him: he left St. Gildas, and went over into Champagne ".

From thence he acquainted Heloifa of his intentions. — She who, fince her retirement from the world, had heard nothing of him, but what fame had reported, received his invitation to the Paraclet with rapture. How enchanting the reflection, that fhe was not forgotten by the man fhe loved; and that fhe fhould be fuccoured by him, when no other friend appeared, and the earth had not an afylum for her! In the thought were abforbed all her cares, and all the neglectful treatment of Abeillard. To her companions fhe communicated the joyful news: they acceded to her propofal, and immediately departed for the Paraclet. — In the number, which was eight, were Agnes and Agatha, two nieces of Abeillard ".

The reader may pleafe his imagination, in picturing to himfelf the firft interview betwixt

" Hift. Calam. " Vie d'Abeil. p. 274. Notz Querect.

BOOK IV.

Abeillard and Heloifa. No two perſons, who had once been lovers, ever met in leſs accordant characters. He, cold as marble, ſtern from philoſophy, ſore from ill-uſage, broken by affliction, and religious, becauſe the hand of fate had made him ſo. His misfortunes had alſo preyed upon his cheek, and he was no more the airy, the handſome, the ſprightly Abeillard, who had animated the gayeſt circles of Paris. — On the other hand, Heloiſa, who was but yet in her eight-and-twentieth year, had loſt little of her former charms: the veil had not disfigured her features, nor had retirement given any harſhneſs to the tone of her mind : ſhe was gentle as ſhe had ever been, and what encroachments, either care, or years, or application had made, were at this moment compenſated . by the inward glow, which the ſight of Abeillard excited, and which beamed upon her countenance, in every expreſſion of joy, of gratitude, of benevolence, of love. — He ſhowed her the ſituation of the Paraclet, the cell where he had dwelt, the other habitations which his ſcholars had conſtructed, and the temple they had raiſed. Theſe, and whatever elſe, from the donations of his friends, he could call his own, in lands or other poſſeſſions, he made over to Heloiſa, and he confirmed them to her and her ſucceſſors, for ever, by a ſolemn donation [u]. She was then

[u] Hiſt. Calam.

unanimouſly

unanimoufly chofen abbefs of the new eftablifhment;
and the little community, difpofing of itfelf in
the moft commodious manner, entered on their
various duties.

Abeillard viewed, with pleafure, this commencement of a rifing family; and having
exhorted them to piety, and to concord, and
to the faithful obfervance of their rule, which
was that of St. Bennet, as they had brought it
from Argenteuil, he took his leave, and returned
to St. Gildas.

Great were the diftreffes, to which Heloifa and
her fifters were, at firft, expofed: they were poor,
and the Paraclet could not fupply them with the
common neceffaries of life. Cheerfully, however,
they fubmitted to their fate, and they practifed,
as they could, the duties of their profeffion, looking up to him for fupport, who nourifhes the
brood of the raven, which calls to him for food.
Heloifa alfo, in the fame fubmiffion of mind, drew
additional confolation from every object, with
which was joined the dear recollection of Abeillard. But foon their wants were relieved. The
neighbouring people, whom the pious behaviour
of the holy fifterhood edified, and whom their
diftreffes moved to compaffion, came in to their
affiftance [11]. Nor were they fatisfied to adminifter
a mere temporary relief: Milo, lord of Nogent,

[11] Hift. Calam.

gave them three farms, and a confiderable portion of land, which lay near to their inclofure; he alfo allowed them to cut down, in his foreft, fuch wood, as they might want for firing or for building. Soon after his niece profeffed herfelf a nun at the Paraclet, when Milo increafed his benefactions, and granted them a right of fifhery in the river, which ran near their convent. —To thefe donations others were added by the nobility of the country. Matilda, countefs of Champagne, was particularly liberal; and even Lewis, king of France, would be numbered amongft their benefactors. The Paraclet was not then fubject to his laws; but he granted the nuns permiffion to buy and fell in his dominions, without paying any duties to himfelf or fucceffors, for ever[16]. — Such liberal and unfolicited contributions fhow the character of the times.

"In a fingle year, fays Abeillard, they acquired "greater poffeffions, than would have fallen into "my hands, had I labored a hundred on the "fpot[17]." This good fortune he particularly afcribes to the powerful efficacy of female diftrefs. As nature has formed women weak, and little able to provide for their own wants, their petitions, he thinks, are more apt to move us; and their virtue, if fuffering, is an object, which challenges the

[16] Quercet. ex Tab. Paraclet. [17] Hift. Calam.

regard of God and men. " But fo many were the
" attractions, continues he, which, in the eyes of
" every beholder, divine providence gave to
" Heloifa, that bifhops viewed her as a daughter,
" abbots as a fifter, and the laity loved her as a
" mother. Her piety, her prudence, her patience,
" her gentlenefs of character, commanded univer-
" fal admiration. Seldom fhe appeared in public;
" the retirement of her cell was better adapted to
" holy meditation and to prayer: but her fociety
" was ardently fought for., and ftrangers wifhed
" to be improved by her edifying converfation."

It is the delineation of a perfect character; but
let it be obferved, that this is the firft time, that
Abeillard has fpoken of Heloifa and of her conduct,
in terms of approbation. Her behaviour at the
Paraclet muft have pleafed him well, and I conceive
the portrait to be faithful. To praife too freely
was not his difpofition, and flattery, he feems,
to have cautioufly referved for himfelf. Heloifa
was as wax in his hands, and to all his inclinations
fhe would mould her foul. When fhe faw that he
was an altered man; that he was pious, referved,
meditative, and religioufly fevere, at once fhe
adopted his maxims, and fhe appeared a finifhed
pattern of monaftic perfection. There were
moments, I believe, when grace was not fo,
triumphant: love and nature would fometimes,

Abeillard is
again cen-
fured.

prevail; and we fhall fee how reluctantly they furrendered a heart, which feemed made to be poffeffed by them alone.

Whilft the Paraclet was in diftrefs, Abeillard had not neglected it. He was often informed of their fituation, and was fometimes blamed by the gentlemen in the neighbourhood, that he did not fufficiently exert his abilities in their fupport: would he preach publicly, and declare their wants, there was little doubt, they faid, of the moft flattering fuccefs". Repeatedly therefore he had gone over to them; and now when fortune began to fmile, and the Paraclet attracted the notice of the charitable and the opulent, he did not difcontinue his vifits. How delightful to him was this fpot, which he had always loved! But when he compared the gentle manners, the innocent converfation: the docile fubmiffion, and the attentive folicitude of his nuns, with the boifterous and untoward deportment of the monks of St. Gildas, it was natural he fhould leave the Paraclet with regret, and fhould return to it with ardor. — He had projected a fcheme, it feems, of paffing much of his time with them : he would attend to the due adminiftration of their temporal concerns, he would inftruct, and he would edify them. " And fince, fays he, the inceffant oppofition of my own

" Hift. Calam.

" fubjects became fo infufferable, I thought, I

" could fometimes withdraw from the tumultuary
" fcene, and breathe the ferene air of this charming
" folitude. I fhould not be ufelefs to them; my
" prefence even might be occafionally neceffary ". "

Thefe vifits of Abeillard to the Paraclet were
foon noticed by his enemies. Innocent furely they
were, and, in many regards, laudable; but they
could be mifconftrued, and malevolence would
not lofe the fatisfaction of indulging her favorite
purfuit. " The eunuch is not quite fo infenfible,
" as we imagined, faid they: the trees, the brooks,
" the whifpering zephyrs of the Paraclet are
" indeed charming, and Abeillard is charitable and
" humane; but fince Heloifa has been there, we
" can hardly count his vifits: may it be that
" Fulbert's niece has yet fome charms for the pious
" folitary "!"

The malicious infinuation reached the ears of
Abeillard, and he was ftill too irritable to difregard
it. Again he entered on a tedious exculpation of
himfelf; and from ancient authorities undertook
to prove, that fuch beings as himfelf were always
accounted harmlefs. His fate, he thought, was
peculiarly hard. But if the mere affociating with
women could be deemed criminal, not our Saviour,
or his apoftles, or the primitive fathers, fhould

---

¹⁹ Hift. Calam.   ²⁰ Ibid.

BOOK
IV.

have efcaped reprehenfion. It was from the example of Jerom only that he could derive confolation: he, like himfelf, had been defamed ; why then fhould he murmur[41].—His adverfaries laughed at his defence, and only repeated their reflections. The difconfolate man could withftand them no longer; he fighed, and with a heavy heart, returned once more into Britany , refolved to fubmit to his cruel deftiny, and to turn his back for ever on the fair inhabitants of the Paraclet[42].

He fettles at St. Gildas , and is perfecuted by his monks.

To cheer, as far as might be, the melancholy hours, and that St. Gildas might not be the grave of his talents, as it was of his peace of mind , he undertook to difcufs certain theological fubjects, which were afterwards publifhed, and of which I fhall have occafion to fpeak.—The refractory monks perfevered in their lawlefs exceffes ; and at once provoked that Abeillard fhould be refolute not to defert his poft, and that he even feemed capable of indulging his favorite purfuits, in the midft of their clamors , they meditated higher fchemes of vengeance. They had recourfe to poifon, which they mixed up with the difhes, or threw into the liquors, which were prepared for his table. By good fortune , or by addrefs , he efcaped thefe nefarious machinations.—They then attempted to poifon the chalice ; which, held the wine for the

[41] Hift. Calam.   [42] Vie d'Abeil. p. 296.

facrifice of the altar: but in this alfo they failed of fuccefs [1]. Among the monks he had friends, who were careful to give him timely notice of the defigns of his enemies. — From the circumftance of the poifoned *chalice*, we difcover that Abeillard was, at this time, a prieft. When he took holy orders is uncertain, though it probably happened whilft he was at St. Denys, foon after his admiffion into that convent.

Conon, count of Nantes, being dangeroufly ill, had requefted Abeillard to come over to him. He obeyed the fummons, taking with him only one fervant, and a young monk, whom he much efteemed. In preference to the count's palace, Abeillard chofe a more humble dwelling : he had a brother living at Nantes, and with him he lodged. Here it was that the fervant, whom the monks had corrupted before he left St. Gildas, attempted to execute another fcheme they had laid to poifon their abbot. They had judged that, at fo great a diftance, he would fufpect no ftratagem, and that at laft they fhould be fuccefsful. The difh was prepared; but when it was laid before his mafter, either from want of appetite, or as he himfelf remarks, by the care of divine providence, he was not difpofed to eat. The young monk was not equally protected; he ate, was foon after feized with convulfions, and expired in extreme torture.

[1] Hift. Calam.

R 4

The fervant inftantly difappeared; from which it
was evident, who had been the perpetrator of the
horrid deed ". — Abeillard remained fome time
longer at Nantes: it was almoft his native fpot,
and here his name was in great eftimation; but
after the count's recovery, he judged proper to
return to his abbey.

As the atrocious defigns of the monks were now
publicly known, Abeillard was advifed to be more
on his guard: he withdrew therefore, with a few
companions, to fome cells at a diftance, where,
it was imagined, he would be more fecure. But
fuch enemies, as were the monks of St. Gildas,
are not eafily deterred from a fixed purpofe:
they followed Abeillard to his cells. Here they
watched his motions; and whenever they were
told that he had ventured to move from home,
they waited his return; and they pofted affaffins
near the roads through which he was to pafs. Nor
were thefe attempts more fuccefsful. A favorite
indeed of heaven muft have been the man, whom
fuch repeated attacks could never, in the leaft,
injure! But, as ufual, I fufpect the tale to be
exaggerated.

An accident, however, foon befel him, which
proved that he was not at leaft invulnerable. Riding
out, one day, for amufement, or on bufinefs, his
horfe violently threw him, by which his neck was

" Hift. Calam.

diflocated. He was relieved by immediate afliftance; but the confequences of his fall, he complains, were very painful, and they caufed a general debility, from which he never quite recovered[11].

No fooner was he able to move about, than he refolved, feeing not the moft gentle ufage could mollify their fury, nor the utmoft caution guard him any longer from their infults, to try on his enemies the effects of canonical cenfures. In an ignorant age, thefe have been fometimes known to fucceed, when other arms have failed. He excommunicated the moft refractory. Intimidated by the fentence, their arrogant effrontery feemed difpofed to relent: they acquainted their abbot, that voluntarily they would leave St. Gildas, and never more give him the fmalleft difturbance, if he would withdraw the cenfure he had pronounced. Abeillard accepted their propofal; to comply with which they folemnly bound themfelves by an oath. But fuch ties would avail little; they did not quit St. Gildas, and very foon recommenced their wonted career of profligacy and bafe intrigue. Abeillard refolved to have recourfe to Rome.

Innocent the fecond was then pope. To him the behaviour of thefe unruly mifcreants was ftated, and he difpatched a minifter, with legatine

[11] Hift. Calam.

powers, whofe duty it fhould be, on the fpot, to examine the truth of the charges, and to pronounce fentence. Before the duke of Britany and the neighbouring prelates the caufe was heard: the criminality of the monks was notorious; and the legate compelled them, again upon oath, to fubfcribe to the former conditions. The bufinefs feemed terminated, and the Roman envoy departed ".

After the departure of the moft factious members, Abeillard came out from his retirement: he prefumed, that all danger was over, and that, in confidence, he might refume the government of his abbey. He was miftaken: the remaining part of the community, either poffeffed all the animofity, or they were difpofed to take up the quarrel, of their exiled brethren. What poifon, and the fword of hired affaffins, had not effected, they doubted not could be executed by their own arm. In the night-time, with daggers in their hands, they affailed his apartments: he was awakened by the noife, and had time to efcape. A fubterraneous paffage offered him an afylum, through which he paffed, and was received into the houfe of a neighbouring gentleman ". This is a forced tranflation of the paffage; the truth is, that they were only meditating this dark fcheme, when

" Hift. Calam. " Vie d'Abeil. t. li. p. 14.

Abeillard was apprized of it, and by the friendly
affiftance of a certain nobleman was refcued from
the danger, which threatened him ".

A more deplorable ftate than this will not eafily
be conceived; and the life of Abeillard feemed to
be winding up in the true form of tragedy: his
mind was not equal to the preffure of circumftances,
and his lamentations are all drawn in character.
" The evils which furround me, fays he; thicken
" every hour, and I fee the naked fword fufpended
" over my head. How like am I to the deluded
" courtier of the Sicilian tyrant! With the
" wealth and gaudy pageantry of royalty before
" him, he viewed the dagger pointed at his life,
" and at once the dream of happinefs was over.
" From the lowly condition of a poor monk I
" was raifed to wealth and honors; and thus it
" ends: my mifery has increafed with my prefer-
" ment. Let my example be a warning to
" thofe, whom ambition may prompt to venture
" fpontaneoufly on the treacherous path of wordly
" grandeur."—Then in the moft religious fentiment
he proceeds. " But fince all things happen by the
" divine appointment; in every diftrefs this fhould
" be the chriftian's confolation, that the goodnefs of
" heaven permits nothing to derange its all-perfect
" fyftem; from evil good is ultimately deduced.
" Let this be our prayer : *Thy will be done !*

" Hift. Calam.

" How inordinately, therefore, do they act who
" confefs that the hand of God directs all events, yet
" murmur when they fuffer : it is their own will
" which they look to, whatever their words may
" be; and in feeking that, they tacitly oppofe
" the unerring ways of providence ". "

In thefe fentiments, which became the abbot of
St. Gildas, he purpofed ftill to remain at his
convent, hoping that time, and lenient meafures,
might at laft give fuccefs to his exertions. In the
fame fentiments it was, that he wrote the
memoirs of his own life, which are brought up
to this period, and here they clofe, about the
year 1134.

" Hift. Calam.

END OF THE FIRST VOLUME.

www.ingramcontent.com/pod-product-compliance
Lightning Source LLC
Chambersburg PA
CBHW031359270326
41929CB00010BA/1253